Master Vue.js in 6 Days

Become a Vue.js Expert in Under a Week

Eric Sarrion

Apress®

Master Vue.js in 6 Days: Become a Vue.js Expert in Under a Week

Eric Sarrion
VIRY CHATILLON, France

ISBN-13 (pbk): 979-8-8688-0363-5   ISBN-13 (electronic): 979-8-8688-0364-2
https://doi.org/10.1007/979-8-8688-0364-2

Copyright © 2024 by Eric Sarrion

Managing Director, Apress Media LLC: Welmoed Spahr
Acquisitions Editor: James Robinson-Prior
Development Editor: James Markham
Coordinating Editor: Gryffin Winkler

Cover designed by eStudioCalamar

Cover image by Photo by Scott Webb on Unsplash (www.unsplash.com)

Distributed to the book trade worldwide by Apress Media, LLC, 1 New York Plaza, New York, NY 10004, U.S.A. Phone 1-800-SPRINGER, fax (201) 348-4505, e-mail orders-ny@springer-sbm.com, or visit www.springeronline.com. Apress Media, LLC is a California LLC and the sole member (owner) is Springer Science + Business Media Finance Inc (SSBM Finance Inc). SSBM Finance Inc is a **Delaware** corporation.

For information on translations, please e-mail booktranslations@springernature.com; for reprint, paperback, or audio rights, please e-mail bookpermissions@springernature.com.

Apress titles may be purchased in bulk for academic, corporate, or promotional use. eBook versions and licenses are also available for most titles. For more information, reference our Print and eBook Bulk Sales web page at http://www.apress.com/bulk-sales.

Any source code or other supplementary material referenced by the author in this book is available to readers on GitHub (https://github.com/Apress). For more detailed information, please visit https://www.apress.com/gp/services/source-code.

If disposing of this product, please recycle the paper

Table of Contents

About the Author

Eric Sarrion is a trainer, a web developer, and an independent consultant. He has been involved in all kinds of IT projects for over 30 years. He is also a long-time author of web development technologies and is renowned for the clarity of his explanations and examples. He resides in Paris, France. Some of his recent publications include *Master React in 5 Days* (Apress), *ChatGPT for Beginners* (Apress), and *JavaScript from Frontend to Backend* (Packt).

About the Technical Reviewer

Fabio Claudio Ferracchiati is a senior consultant and analyst/developer using Microsoft technologies. He works for Bluarancio (`www.bluarancio.com`). He is a Microsoft Certified Solution Developer as well as a Microsoft Certified Application Developer for .NET, a Microsoft Certified Professional, and a prolific author and technical reviewer. Over the past ten years, he's written articles for Italian and international magazines and coauthored more than ten books on a variety of computer topics.

Introduction

Welcome to the exciting world of Vue.js! You are holding in your hands a comprehensive guide to mastering this JavaScript framework in just six days. Whether you are a novice developer seeking a solid starting point or a seasoned professional looking to deepen your skills, this book is tailored for you.

Vue.js has emerged as one of the most popular and revered JavaScript frameworks in the web development industry. Its simplicity, flexibility, and outstanding performance have made it a preferred choice for creating modern web applications, be it small interactive applications or large-scale projects.

This book is structured into six days of learning, each focusing on key aspects of Vue.js. You will embark on a progressive journey, from creating components to handling events, delving into HTTP requests, custom directives, and composables. Each day will bring you new skills and practical knowledge that you can immediately apply to your projects.

What will you find within these pages? Clear explanations, concrete examples, hands-on exercises, and development tips. We will guide you through the fundamental concepts of Vue.js and assist you in becoming a proficient Vue.js developer.

Prepare for an exciting journey. Whether it's for creating professional web applications or simply expanding your horizons in web development, this book will equip you with the necessary skills to excel in the world of Vue.js. So dive into this adventure and become a Vue.js master in just six days!

CHAPTER 1

Day 1: Mastering Components in Vue.js

Welcome to Chapter 1 of our journey to master Vue.js in just six days. During this first day, we will delve into the world of Vue.js, starting by understanding why it is so powerful and exploring its key concept, the Virtual DOM. We will then follow a step-by-step process to create our first Vue.js application, guiding you through the installation of Node.js and Vue CLI, as well as examining the default files generated in a Vue.js application.

We will also explore the structure of a Vue.js application, examining configuration files, directories, and essential components. Additionally, we will demonstrate how to break down an application into Vue.js components, adhering to naming conventions and creating our first component.

Finally, we will delve into fundamental aspects such as reactivity usage, defining methods and computed properties in a Vue.js component, and managing the lifecycle.

© Eric Sarrion 2024
E. Sarrion, *Master Vue.js in 6 Days*, https://doi.org/10.1007/979-8-8688-0364-2_1

Why Use Vue.js

When it comes to choosing a JavaScript framework for modern and interactive web development, Vue.js stands out among the most popular and compelling choices. With its simple and reactive approach, Vue.js offers a smooth and enjoyable development experience, suitable for both beginners and experienced developers.

In this section, we will explore five essential reasons why Vue.js is a wise choice for your development projects. From its ease of learning to optimal performance, innovative Composition API, and dynamic ecosystem, let's quickly discover why Vue.js rightfully deserves its place among modern development frameworks.

We will, of course, have the opportunity to explore these different facets in depth later in the book.

1. **Ease of Learning and Implementation**

   Vue.js is renowned for its gentle learning curve. Its simple and declarative syntax, along with comprehensive and user-friendly documentation, makes it an excellent choice for both novice web developers and experienced professionals. Concepts such as components, directives, and composables are intuitive and easy to grasp, speeding up the learning and development process.

2. **Reactivity and Efficient Rendering**

   Reactivity is at the core of Vue.js. With its bidirectional data binding system and the ability to track changes in the application's state, Vue.js ensures reactive and efficient rendering. User interface updates are handled optimally, resulting in a smooth and performant user experience, even for complex applications.

3. **Composition API for Better Code Organization**

   With the introduction of the Composition API (starting from Vue.js version 3, as used in this book), Vue.js provides a more structured and modular way to organize code. Instead of dividing logic by options in components (as proposed in Vue.js version 2), the Composition API allows grouping logic by functionality, making the code more readable, maintainable, and scalable. It also facilitates logic sharing between components.

4. **Extensive Ecosystem of Libraries and Tools**

   Vue.js benefits from a dynamic ecosystem composed of many third-party libraries and complementary tools. Whether it's state management with Vuex, routing with Vue Router, or integration with other libraries and frameworks, Vue.js offers flexible options to meet various development needs.

5. **Optimal Performance and Lightweight Size**

   Vue.js is designed to be lightweight and fast. With its compact size and optimized performance, Vue.js applications load quickly in the browser, enhancing the overall user experience. Additionally, Vue.js allows server-side rendering (SSR) for even better performance in terms of SEO and initial loading time.

   Vue.js distinguishes itself through its simplicity, reactivity, flexibility, performance, and ecosystem, making it a wise choice for developing modern and dynamic web applications.

3

Virtual DOM

The Virtual DOM (Document Object Model) is a key concept in many modern JavaScript frameworks, including Vue.js. It is a lightweight and efficient abstraction of the real DOM, which represents the structure of a web page in the browser's memory. The goal of the Virtual DOM is to improve performance and the efficiency of DOM updates by minimizing direct manipulations, which can be time-consuming.

Let's now explore how the binding between the browser's DOM and Vue.js's Virtual DOM works.

Step 1: Virtual DOM Operation

Here's how the Virtual DOM operates in Vue.js:

1. **Virtual DOM Creation**: When a Vue.js component is created, it generates an internal Virtual DOM that reflects the current structure of the DOM. This Virtual DOM is a virtual and lightweight copy of the actual DOM tree.

2. **Initial Rendering**: At startup, the component generates the Virtual DOM using the data and templates defined in the Vue.js code.

3. **Change Detection**: When a component's data changes (due to user interaction, such as clicking a button), Vue.js uses a process called "reactivity" to detect data changes. This triggers a Virtual DOM update process.

4. **Comparison and Update**: Once data changes are detected, Vue.js compares the new state of the Virtual DOM with the previous state, identifying differences between the two versions.

5. **Patch Generation**: Vue.js generates a set of instructions (reconciliation process) describing the modifications to be made to the real DOM to reflect the changes. These instructions are created efficiently, minimizing the number of direct DOM manipulations.

6. **DOM Update**: Finally, Vue.js applies the reconciliation process to the real DOM in an optimized manner. Only the parts of the DOM that have changed are updated, significantly reducing performance compared to a full DOM update.

The major contribution of the Virtual DOM lies in the efficiency and speed of updates. Instead of directly manipulating the DOM with each data change, Vue.js uses the Virtual DOM to minimize actual DOM modifications, resulting in improved performance and a better user experience. This allows developers to focus on application logic rather than complex DOM manipulations. Vue.js's Virtual DOM is therefore a crucial technique that optimizes browser performance by intelligently detecting changes and efficiently updating the DOM, enhancing reactivity and the user experience.

Step 2: Concrete Example

Here is a concrete example to illustrate how the Virtual DOM works in Vue.js through a simple case: incrementing a counter by clicking a button.

Suppose we have a Vue.js component called MyCounter that displays a counter and a button to increment it. Here is how it could be implemented (this code example will be explained later in this chapter; the key here is to explain how the DOM is updated with each click on the "Increment" button). The MyCounter component is associated with a MyCounter.vue file described as follows:

File MyCounter.vue

```
<script setup>
import { ref } from "vue";

const count = ref(0);
const increment = () => count.value++

</script>

<template>
  <div>
    <p>Counter: {{ count }}</p>
    <button @click="increment()">Increment</button>
  </div>
</template>
```

This component is displayed in a browser as follows:

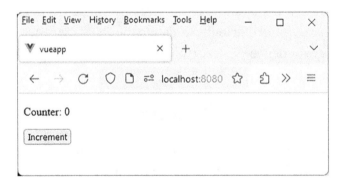

Figure 1-1. *First display of the Vue.js application*

Upon clicking the "Increment" button once, the counter value increments from 0 to 1:

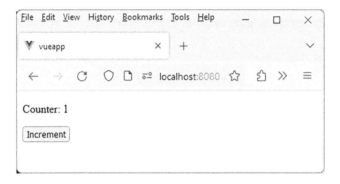

Figure 1-2. *Incrementing the counter from 0 to 1*

Let's examine how Vue.js's Virtual DOM handles updates when clicking the button to increment the counter:

1. Upon startup, the MyCounter component is mounted, and the Virtual DOM is created based on the template and initial data.

2. When clicking the "Increment" button, the increment() method is called. This changes the value of the count variable in the component.

3. Vue.js detects the data change through its reactivity system.

4. The Virtual DOM is updated to reflect the new value of count. Vue.js compares the old and new Virtual DOM to determine differences.

5. Vue.js generates a set of instructions describing the modification to be made to the real DOM. In this case, the instructions simply indicate that the counter text should be updated.

6. The real DOM is updated with the executed instructions. Only the part of the DOM corresponding to the counter is modified, minimizing direct DOM manipulations.

This example illustrates how Vue.js's Virtual DOM optimizes DOM updates by detecting changes, then generating efficient instructions to selectively update the real DOM. This provides a reactive user experience while optimizing performance.

Creating a First Vue.js Application

Creating a Vue.js application requires installing the Vue CLI utility, downloadable after installing the npm utility from the Node.js server.

Step 1: Installing Node.js and Vue CLI

Ensure that you have Node.js installed on your system, which you can download from the official Node.js website (https://nodejs.org/). Next, install Vue CLI using the npm install -g @vue/cli command in your terminal:

Figure 1-3. *Vue CLI installation*

Once Vue CLI is installed, you can use the vue create command to create the Vue.js application.

Step 2: Creating the Vue.js Application

After installing Vue CLI, you can create a new Vue.js project by running the command vue create vueapp. This will create the vueapp application in the newly created vueapp directory:

Figure 1-4. *Creating the Vue.js application with Vue CLI*

The system prompts for the desired version of Vue.js. We retain the default selection of the current version 3 by pressing the Enter key on the keyboard.

The Vue.js application named vueapp begins to be created:

Figure 1-5. *Creating the Vue.js application in progress*

Once the application creation process is complete, it will be displayed on the screen:

Figure 1-6. *Completion of Vue.js application creation*

Once the Vue.js application is created, the next step is to start it.

Step 3: Launching the Vue.js Application

To start the previously created Vue.js application, simply type the two commands in the terminal window as indicated: cd vueapp, then npm run serve.

Figure 1-7. *Launching the Vue.js application*

The npm run serve command starts a Node.js server on which the Vue.js application will run.

Once the Node.js server is launched, the terminal screen becomes the following:

Figure 1-8. *Completion of the server launch process with the Vue.js application*

The terminal window indicates that the Vue.js application is accessible at the URL http://localhost:8080.

Let's enter this URL in a browser:

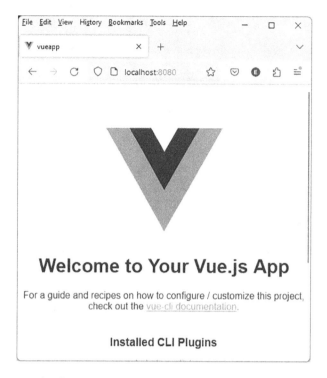

Figure 1-9. *Default Vue.js application created*

We now have access to the previously created Vue.js application.

Analyzing the Files Created by Default in the Vue.js Application

The vue create vueapp command created a vueapp directory containing configuration files and directories containing the source code for our Vue.js application.

Figure 1-10. *Contents of the "vueapp" directory in the Vue.js application*

We can see that the Vue.js application directory primarily contains configuration files and three main directories (node_modules, public, and src). Let's now explain their role and contents.

Step 1: Configuration Files (with .js and .json Extensions)

The configuration files are directly attached to the root of the application. They serve, among other things, to enable the execution of the Vue.js application on a Node.js server. For example, here is the content of the package.json file, which is traditionally used to configure an application to run on a Node.js server:

File package.json

```
{
  "name": "vueapp",
  "version": "0.1.0",
  "private": true,
```

```json
"scripts": {
  "serve": "vue-cli-service serve",
  "build": "vue-cli-service build",
  "lint": "vue-cli-service lint"
},
"dependencies": {
  "core-js": "^3.8.3",
  "vue": "^3.2.13"
},
"devDependencies": {
  "@babel/core": "^7.12.16",
  "@babel/eslint-parser": "^7.12.16",
  "@vue/cli-plugin-babel": "~5.0.0",
  "@vue/cli-plugin-eslint": "~5.0.0",
  "@vue/cli-service": "~5.0.0",
  "eslint": "^7.32.0",
  "eslint-plugin-vue": "^8.0.3"
},
"eslintConfig": {
  "root": true,
  "env": {
    "node": true
  },
  "extends": [
    "plugin:vue/vue3-essential",
    "eslint:recommended"
  ],
  "parserOptions": {
    "parser": "@babel/eslint-parser"
  },
  "rules": {}
```

```
  },
  "browserslist": [
    "> 1%",
    "last 2 versions",
    "not dead",
    "not ie 11"
  ]
}
```

In this file, you'll find the list of dependencies that our application needs to run, along with their respective versions.

The "scripts" key allows the execution of commands such as npm run serve, which launches the development server on port 8080.

Additional scripts can be added. For example, let's insert a new script "start" in the "scripts" section that starts the Vue.js application on port 3000 instead of the default port 8080.

Adding the "start" script (package.json file)

```
"scripts": {
    "serve": "vue-cli-service serve",
    "start": "vue-cli-service serve --port 3000",
    "build": "vue-cli-service build",
    "lint": "vue-cli-service lint"
},
```

The command npm run start starts the server on port 3000.

Figure 1-11. *Execution of the "start" script*

The Vue.js application is now accessible at the URL http://localhost:3000, thanks to the server launched on port 3000.

We briefly examined the configuration files of the Vue.js application. Let's now look at the application directories, starting with the node_modules directory.

Step 2: node_modules Directory

The node_modules directory contains external dependencies necessary for the proper functioning of the Vue.js application (those specified in the package.json file), as well as other libraries and modules that may be added to the project later.

Here is a partial content of this directory shortly after creating the application.

.bin	ajv-formats
.cache	ajv-keywords
@aashutoshrathi	ansi-colors
@achrinza	ansi-escapes
@ampproject	ansi-html-community
@babel	ansi-regex
@discoveryjs	ansi-styles
@eslint	anymatch
@hapi	any-promise
@humanwhocodes	arch
@jridgewell	argparse
@leichtgewicht	array-flatten
@nicolo-ribaudo	array-union
@node-ipc	astral-regex
@nodelib	async
@polka	at-least-node
@sideway	autoprefixer
@soda	babel-loader

Figure 1-12. *Partial content of the node_modules directory*

Step 3: public Directory

The public directory contains the static files of the application. This public directory typically includes the following two files:

- The favicon.png file, which specifies the application's icon to be displayed in the browser tabs.

- The index.html file, which is the starting file of the Vue.js application.

Let's see the content of the index.html file. This content is rarely modified as it incorporates a crucial <div> HTML element for the functioning of the Vue.js application.

File public/index.html

```
<!DOCTYPE html>
<html lang="">
  <head>
    <meta charset="utf-8">
    <meta http-equiv="X-UA-Compatible" content="IE=edge">
    <meta name="viewport" content="width=device-width,initial-
    scale=1.0">
    <link rel="icon" href="<%= BASE_URL %>favicon.ico">
    <title><%= htmlWebpackPlugin.options.title %></title>
  </head>
  <body>
    <noscript>
      <strong>We're sorry but <%= htmlWebpackPlugin.options.
      title %> doesn't work properly without JavaScript
      enabled. Please enable it to continue.</strong>
    </noscript>
    <div id="app"></div>
    <!-- built files will be auto injected -->
  </body>
</html>
```

The index.html file contains a single <div> element, which has been assigned the default identifier "app". This convention allows us to insert the Vue.js components of our application into this <div> element, visualizing the Vue.js application in the browser. We will see here how this is achieved.

Now let's examine the content of the `src` directory, which will help us understand the purpose of the previous `<div>` element.

Step 4: src Directory

The `src` directory of the application is the most widely used and modified when building our Vue.js applications. It contains the source code for our Vue.js components as well as static files such as images or CSS style files.

It consists of the following files and directories:

Figure 1-13. *Content of the src directory*

Let's examine in detail each file and directory listed in the `src` directory. We'll start with the `main.js` file.

Step 5: src/main.js

The `main.js` file is crucial for starting a Vue.js application. Let's see its content:

File src/main.js

```
import { createApp } from 'vue'
import App from './App.vue'

createApp(App).mount('#app')
```

Here's an explanation of the previous code:

1. The first statement `import { createApp } from 'vue'` imports the `createApp()` function from the "vue" package. The "vue" package is located in the `node_modules` directory of the application. The `createApp()` function will be used later to create a Vue.js application instance.

2. The second statement `import App from './App.vue'` imports the App component from the `App.vue` file. The App component will be the root component of the application.

3. Finally, the statement `createApp(App).mount('#app')` first calls the `createApp(App)` function to create a Vue.js application instance using the previously imported App component. Then the `mount('#app')` method is called on this instance. This mounts the application onto the DOM element with the id `"app"`. This `"app"` element was present in the `index.html` file seen earlier. This element serves as the main container in which the Vue.js application will be displayed.

In summary, the code in the main.js file creates an instance of the Vue.js application using the App component as the root component and then mounts this instance on an element with the id `"app"` in the DOM. This effectively initializes the Vue.js application and makes it ready to be displayed and used in the browser.

Step 6: src/App.vue

We explained previously that the App.vue file is associated with the App component, which will be displayed in the HTML page. The App component describes the structure of our Vue.js application using the syntax provided by the Vue.js framework. Here is the content of the App.vue file:

App component (src/App.vue file)

```
<template>
  <img alt="Vue logo" src="./assets/logo.png">
  <HelloWorld msg="Welcome to Your Vue.js App"/>
</template>

<script>
import HelloWorld from './components/HelloWorld.vue'

export default {
  name: 'App',
  components: {
    HelloWorld
  }
}
</script>

<style>
#app {
  font-family: Avenir, Helvetica, Arial, sans-serif;
  -webkit-font-smoothing: antialiased;
  -moz-osx-font-smoothing: grayscale;
  text-align: center;
  color: #2c3e50;
  margin-top: 60px;
}
</style>
```

The App.vue file is a Vue.js component that defines the structure (<template> section), logic (<script> section), and style (<style> section) of the main part of the application. Here is a concise explanation of the content:

1. **<template> section**

   - The content between the <template> tags defines the HTML structure of the component.

   - It includes an <img> tag displaying a Vue.js logo and a <HelloWorld> component with a "msg" property.

2. **<script> section**

   - The <script> section contains the JavaScript logic of the component.

   - It imports the HelloWorld component from the HelloWorld.vue file.

   - The exported object (via the export default statement) defines the name of the component (here, "App") and the components it uses (in this case, "HelloWorld").

3. **<style> section**

   - The <style> section contains CSS style rules for the component.

   - The element with the id "app" is styled with various CSS properties for formatting the application. Recall that the element with the id "app" is the one on which the Vue.js application is "mounted."

In summary, the `App.vue` file combines HTML structure, JavaScript logic, and CSS styles to define the main component of the application. It imports the `HelloWorld` component and displays a Vue.js logo and a message inside this component. The style is applied to the main container with the id `"app"`. This file forms the visual and functional basis of the application.

This `App.vue` file (associated with the `App` component) will need to be modified later to display our own Vue.js application.

We have described the two main files in the `src` directory, namely, the `main.js` file and the `App.vue` file. We have seen that the `App` component uses another component named `HelloWorld`. This new component is located in the `components` directory of the application. Let's describe the contents of the `components` directory, specifically the `HelloWorld.vue` file associated with the `HelloWorld` component.

Step 7: src/components Directory

The `src/components` directory contains files describing the internal components of our Vue.js application. Subdirectories can be added if a more structured organization is desired.

Let's examine the file currently present in this directory. It is the `HelloWorld.vue` file associated with the `HelloWorld` component.

HelloWorld component (src/components/HelloWorld.vue file)

```
<template>
  <div class="hello">
    <h1>{{ msg }}</h1>
    <p>
      For a guide and recipes on how to configure / customize
      this project,<br>
      check out the
      <a href="https://cli.vuejs.org" target="_blank"
      rel="noopener">vue-cli documentation</a>.
```

```
</p>
<h3>Installed CLI Plugins</h3>
<ul>
  li><a href="https://github.com/vuejs/vue-cli/tree/
  dev/packages/%40vue/cli-plugin-babel" target="_blank"
  rel="noopener">babel</a></li>
  <li><a href="https://github.com/vuejs/vue-cli/tree/
  dev/packages/%40vue/cli-plugin-eslint" target="_blank"
  rel="noopener">eslint</a></li>
</ul>
<h3>Essential Links</h3>
<ul>
  <li><a href="https://vuejs.org" target="_blank"
  rel="noopener">Core Docs</a></li>
  <li><a href="https://forum.vuejs.org" target="_blank"
  rel="noopener">Forum</a></li>
  <li><a href="https://chat.vuejs.org" target="_blank"
  rel="noopener">CommunityChat</a></li>
  <li><a href="https://twitter.com/vuejs" target="_blank"
  rel="noopener">Twitter</a></li>
  <li><a href="https://news.vuejs.org" target="_blank"
  rel="noopener">News</a></li>
</ul>
<h3>Ecosystem</h3>
<ul>
  <li><a href="https://router.vuejs.org" target="_blank"
  rel="noopener">vue-router</a></li>
  <li><a href="https://vuex.vuejs.org" target="_blank"
  rel="noopener">vuex</a></li>
  <li><a href="https://github.com/vuejs/vue-devtools#vue-
  devtools" target="_blank" rel="noopener">
  vue-devtools</a></li>
```

```
    <li><a href="https://vue-loader.vuejs.org"
    target="_blank" rel="noopener">vue-loader</a></li>
    <li><a href="https://github.com/vuejs/awesome-vue"
    target="_blank" rel="noopener">awesome-vue</a></li>
  </ul>
 </div>
</template>

<script>
export default {
  name: 'HelloWorld',
  props: {
    msg: String
  }
}
</script>

<!-- Add "scoped" attribute to limit CSS to this component
only -->
<style scoped>
h3 {
  margin: 40px 0 0;
}
ul {
  list-style-type: none;
  padding: 0;
}
li {
  display: inline-block;
  margin: 0 10px;
}
```

```
a {
  color: #42b983;
}
</style>
```

We find the three sections of a Vue.js component, as we discussed in the previous section when describing the App component:

- The `<template>` section defines the HTML structure of the component.

- The `<script>` section describes the JavaScript logic of the component.

- The `<style>` section describes the styles used in the component. The `scoped` attribute indicated here localizes the styles defined only for the `HelloWorld` component.

We will have the opportunity in the following pages to explain in detail the possible content of a Vue.js component. We already know that it contains the three sections mentioned earlier.

Step 8: src/assets Directory

The `src/assets` directory is used to store static files of the application, such as images or globally applied CSS files for the entire Vue.js application. In our case, it contains only the `logo.png` file corresponding to the image displayed in the Vue.js application.

We have now completed the quick description of each of the files and directories created in the default Vue.js application "vueapp" using the `vue create vueapp` command. We have seen that the files describing our application are mainly located in the `src` directory and its subdirectories.

We will now explain how to design a Vue.js application by breaking it down into different components according to what we want to achieve.

Decomposition of a Vue.js Application into Components

Breaking down an application into components, as Vue.js suggests, is a common approach in software development. This methodology promotes the creation of a modular structure that simplifies code maintenance, reuse, and clarity.

Here is a simple example of breaking down an application into components.

Let's imagine that we want to design an application that displays a list of tasks to be done, each accompanied by a check box to indicate its status (completed or not). To do this, we would start by segmenting the application into two main components: a parent component called "TaskList" and a child component named "TaskItem."

The parent component "TaskList" would be responsible for managing the complete list of tasks to be done. Its responsibility would involve retrieving the list data from a data source (such as an API or a database), performing sorting and filtering operations, and then passing this data to the child component "TaskItem."

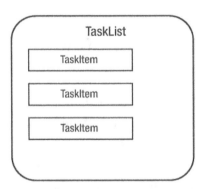

Figure 1-14. *TaskList and TaskItem components*

The child component "TaskItem," on the other hand, would be responsible for displaying an individual task. It would show the task's name and a check box to indicate its status (completed or not). This component would be versatile and display each task whenever it is called by the parent component "TaskList."

Next, we could further fragment the "TaskList" component into subcomponents. For example, "TaskListHeader" could handle the header of the list, "TaskListFooter" the bottom of the list, and "TaskListFilter" the management of filters within the list. Each subcomponent would be responsible for a specific part of the task list, contributing to code clarity and reusability.

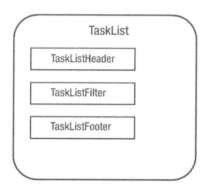

Figure 1-15. *TaskList, TaskListHeader, TaskListFilter, and TaskListFooter components*

Finally, we could also subdivide the "TaskItem" component into additional subcomponents. For example, "TaskName" could focus on displaying the task's name, "TaskCheckbox" on showing the check box, and "TaskDueDate" on displaying the task's due date. Each of these subcomponents would play a specific role in displaying an individual task, bringing more modularity to the design and simplifying code management.

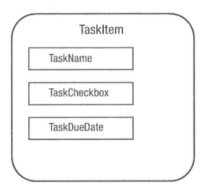

Figure 1-16. *TaskItem, TaskName, TaskCheckbox, and TaskDueDate*
components

By decomposing our application into components, we've established a
modular architecture, simplifying code readability, update management,
and the potential for reuse. Moreover, since each component is responsible
for a well-defined task, the debugging process is greatly facilitated, as each
component can be addressed independently.

Naming Conventions for Vue.js Components

A Vue.js component name is written in PascalCase, with an initial capital
letter for each word in the component's name. To avoid assigning a
component name that might also be associated with an HTML element,
the Vue.js component name must be defined with a minimum of two
words. HTML elements are all defined with a single word, such as `<img>`,
`<p>`, `<span>`, etc. Therefore, if Vue.js component names are defined
with a minimum of two words, there is no risk of confusion with HTML
tag names.

Thus, you can create the `MyCounter` component in Vue.js, but you
cannot create the `Counter` component because it consists of a single word,
while `MyCounter` consists of two words.

The only exception to this rule is the App component, which is the only one written with a single word.

Once the MyCounter component is created, it can be used in the <template> sections as <MyCounter> or <my-counter>. Both forms of writing are equivalent in Vue.js, although the <MyCounter> syntax is recommended.

Creating a First Component with Vue.js

A component is defined using a .vue extension file and must be in the form of components like App and HelloWorld, defined in the App.vue and HelloWorld.vue files described earlier. It will thus include the <script>, <template>, and <style> sections, which will be filled in according to the component's needs. If one of the sections has no elements, it can be omitted. This is often the case for the <style> section.

Here is an example of the MyCounter.vue component, which simply displays the text "MyCounter Component" in an <h1> tag. The MyCounter.vue file will be located in the components directory of the src directory in the application.

File src/components/MyCounter.vue

```
<script>

</script>

<template>

<h1> MyCounter Component </h1>

</template>

<style scoped>

</style>
```

The `<script>` and `<style>` sections are not necessary but are present as they may contain added instructions later. The `MyCounter` component needs to be inserted into the App component to be displayed within it. Indeed, the App component currently uses the `HelloWorld` component seen previously. Let's modify the App component to incorporate the `MyCounter` component.

The App component can be written in two ways, depending on the Vue.js syntax one wishes to use:

- Options API syntax (available from Vue.js version 2)

- Composition API syntax (available from Vue.js version 3)

Using the Options API syntax, the `App.vue` file becomes the following:

Using the Options API syntax (file src/App.vue)

```
<script>
import MyCounter from './components/MyCounter.vue'

export default {
  components : {
    MyCounter : MyCounter
    // As the key and the value are identical, we can also
    write more simply:
    // MyCounter
  }
}

</script>

<template>
  <MyCounter />
</template>

<style scoped>
</style>
```

The `MyCounter.vue` file is imported into the `App` component using the `import` statement in the `<script>` section of the component. Then, the `MyCounter` component is displayed in the `<template>` section using the `<MyCounter />` tag.

In the `<script>` section, we added the `export default` statement of an object with the components option describing the components used in the `App` component. This is the traditional way of using the syntax with options, proposed in version 2 of Vue.js. It is called the Options API syntax.

Another syntax is possible, introduced from version 3 of Vue.js. It is called the Composition API syntax.

Let's use the Composition API syntax to write the `App` component in the `App.vue` file:

Using the Composition API syntax (file src/App.vue)

```
<script setup>
import MyCounter from './components/MyCounter.vue'
</script>

<template>
  <MyCounter />
</template>

<style scoped>
</style>
```

Here, note the `setup` attribute added to the `<script>` element. This attribute in the `<script>` tag allows importing the `MyCounter.vue` file without having to explicitly declare the `MyCounter` component within the `App` component. This is a convenience added in Vue.js version 3, known as the Composition API syntax.

Let's verify that both versions of the `App` component work by displaying the URL `http://localhost:8080`.

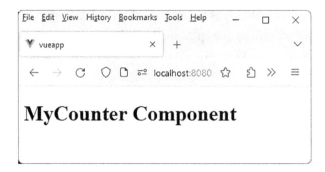

Figure 1-17. *MyCounter Component*

Which syntax, Options API or Composition API, should we use to write a Vue.js component? We will use the Composition API syntax here, as it is newer and simpler to use for writing components.

Defining Styles in a Vue.js Component

Let's modify the style of the <h1> element in the MyCounter component. To do this, simply add a CSS style in the <style> section of the MyCounter component.

Style of the <h1> element (file src/components/MyCounter.vue)

```
<script setup>

</script>

<template>
<h1> MyCounter Component </h1>

</template>

<style scoped>

h1 {
  font-family:papyrus;
```

```
font-size:20px;
}
```

```
</style>
```

The MyCounter component now displays with a new font style.

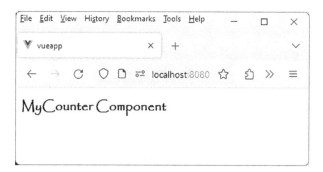

Figure 1-18. *Component MyCounter with a new font style*

Let's now explain the use of the scoped attribute in the <style> tag.

Using the Scoped Attribute in the <style> Tag

The scoped attribute in a <style> tag in Vue.js is used to restrict the scope of CSS styles to a specific component. This means that styles defined within a <style scoped> tag will only apply to elements within the current Vue component and will not propagate to elements in other components.

Here is an example to illustrate the difference between using scoped and not using it:

Without the scoped attribute (file src/components/MyCounter.vue)

```
<template>
  <div>
    <p class="red-text">MyCounter Component</p>
  </div>
```

```
</template>
```

\<style\>
```
.red-text {
  color: red;
}
</style>
```

In this example, the CSS class `.red-text` is defined in the global style of the component. It could potentially impact other components if the class is used elsewhere in the application.

With the scoped attribute (file src/components/MyCounter.vue)

```
<template>
  <div>
    <p class="red-text">MyCounter Component</p>
  </div>
</template>
```

\<style scoped\>
```
.red-text {
  color: red;
}
</style>
```

In this example, the `.red-text` class is defined within a `<style scoped>` tag, indicating that it will only apply to elements within the current component. The styles defined here will have no impact on other components.

The `scoped` attribute is particularly useful for avoiding style conflicts between components and maintaining style isolation. It facilitates the creation of reusable components and simplifies style management in a Vue.js application. Each component can define its styles without concern for styles defined in other components, contributing to better code organization and maintainability.

Using Vue.js DevTools

Vue.js DevTools is a browser extension designed for debugging applications built with Vue.js. Simply search for "Vue.js DevTools" on Google to download it for our browser.

For instance, here is the link for Firefox:

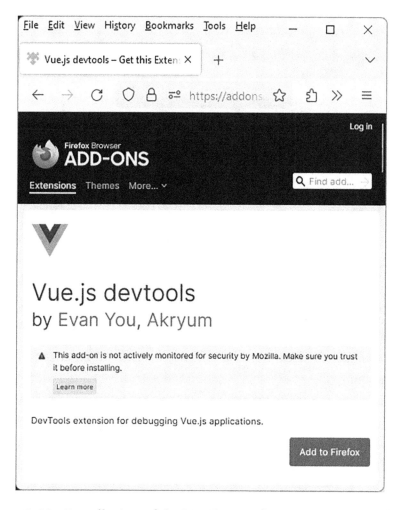

Figure 1-19. *Installation of the Vue DevTools extension on Firefox*

Click the "Add to Firefox" button. Next, display the console by pressing the F12 key on the keyboard. Then, select the Vue menu by clicking >>.

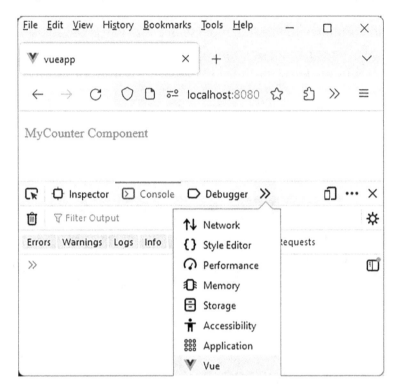

Figure 1-20. *Selection of the Vue DevTools extension*

The console window refreshes, displaying the components used in the application:

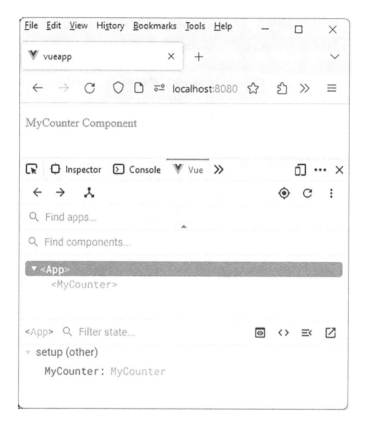

Figure 1-21. *Components of the application displayed in Vue*
DevTools

Using Vue.js Reactivity with the ref( ) Method

Reactivity is a crucial concept when developing applications with Vue.
js. This concept allows for automatic updating of the HTML page display
when a so-called reactive variable is modified in the program.

If a reactive variable is modified by the program, this modification
will be visible wherever the reactive variable is used in the component's
display.

This concept enables the separation of program variables and where they are displayed, as Vue.js takes care of managing the display modification.

A reactive variable is defined within a component and is associated with the component in which it is defined. We create a reactive variable using the ref() method defined in Vue.js. Let's demonstrate how to define and modify a reactive variable with the ref() method. We will use a component called MyCounter, which displays a reactive variable count that increments when a button is clicked.

In all the following examples, the App component, which incorporates the MyCounter component, is as described here:

App component (file src/App.vue)

```
<script setup>
import MyCounter from './components/MyCounter.vue'
</script>

<template>
  <MyCounter />
</template>
```

We use the Composition API syntax to define and use a reactive variable count that increments upon clicking a button labeled "count+1". The Composition API of Vue.js defines the ref() method, which we will employ.

The MyCounter component is written as follows:

MyCounter component (file src/components/MyCounter.vue)

```
<script setup>

import { ref } from "vue";

// Creating a reactive variable count with an initial
value of 0
```

```
const count = ref(0);
```

```
</script>
```

```
<template>
```

```
<h3>MyCounter Component</h3>
```

```
Reactive variable count: <b>{{ count }}</b>
<br /><br />
<button @click="count++">count+1</button>
```

```
</template>
```

The Composition API is used here within the `<script setup>` syntax. The `ref()` method, defined in Vue.js, is usable because it is imported with the statement `import { ref } from "vue"`. All Vue.js methods used in our programs must be imported in this manner before they can be utilized. A slight variation of this syntax is explained in the following section.

The reactive variable `count` is created and initialized with the statement `count = ref(value)`. Subsequently, the `count` variable can be used in the `<template>` section, as mentioned earlier. Let's display the URL `http://localhost:8080` in the browser:

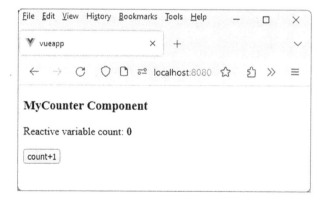

Figure 1-22. *Usage of a reactive variable "count"*

Let's click multiple times the "count+1" button:

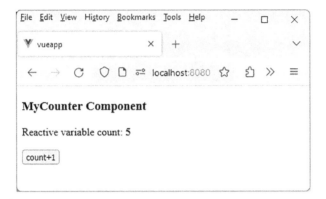

Figure 1-23. *Incrementing the reactive variable "count"*

The variable count is indeed reactive as it is modified with each click on the "count+1" button.

Notice that the incrementation of the count variable is performed directly in the <template> section by writing the <button> element as follows:

Incrementation of the reactive variable count (file src/components/ MyCounter.vue)

```
<button @click="count++">count+1</button>
```

The operation performed here is simple and corresponds to the "count++" instruction. However, in more complex scenarios, it would be more appropriate to use a function call to perform the corresponding processing.

Importing Vue.js Methods into Our Programs

The use of the `ref()` method requires writing the statement `import { ref } from "vue"`, where the curly braces contain the list of methods used in the JavaScript code.

Alternatively, one can perform a global import of all Vue.js methods without having to enumerate them in the list. This can be achieved using the statement `import * as vue from "vue"`. The variable name used after the `"as"` keyword is arbitrary but must be used in the subsequent JavaScript code. Let's rewrite the previous program following this principle:

Using import * as vue from "vue" (file src/components/MyCounter.vue)

```
<script setup>

import * as vue from "vue";

// Creating a reactive variable count with an initial
value of 0
const count = vue.ref(0);

</script>

<template>

<h3>MyCounter Component</h3>

Reactive variable count: <b>{{ count }}</b>
<br /><br />
<button @click="count++">count+1</button>

</template>
```

We observe that the statement `ref(0)` needs to be prefixed with the variable "vue", so it is written as `vue.ref(0)`. In this instance, we chose to use the variable name "vue", but it can be any variable name.

Defining Methods in a Vue.js Component

We've seen how to create reactive variables in the component using the `ref(value)` method. It's also possible to create methods in a component that can be used in the `<template>` section of the component.

Previously, we wrote the processing to be executed after clicking the button directly in the value of the `@click` attribute. Instead of specifying the `count++` instruction, we can replace it with a method call, for example, `increment()`. Thus, we would write `@click="increment()"` instead of `@click="count++"`.

Let's explore how to define and use methods using the Composition API syntax.

Definition of the increment() method (file src/components/ MyCounter.vue)

```
<script setup>

import { ref } from "vue";

// Creating a reactive variable count with an initial
value of 0
const count = ref(0);

function increment() {
   count.value++;   // One accesses the value of count using
                    count.value
}

</script>
```

```
<template>

<h3>MyCounter Component</h3>

Reactive variable count: <b>{{ count }}</b>
<br /><br />
<button @click="increment()">count+1</button>

</template>
```

Functions are defined in the `<script setup>` section of the component. Functions defined in this section will then be accessible in the `<template>` section of the component.

Accessing the reactive variable `count` defined by `count = ref(0)` is done using the `value` property of the reactive variable `count`, namely, `count.value`.

Note that the variable `count` can be defined using the `const` keyword because it remains constant (its value, representing a reference to an object in memory, does not change). It is the `value` property of this object that is modified.

Let's verify that everything works in the same manner:

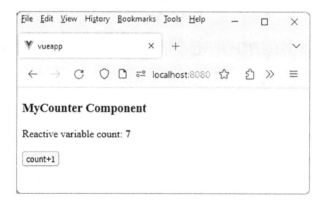

Figure 1-24. *Usage of methods in a component*

Note that the `increment()` function can also be defined using the ES6 syntax. Instead of:

Traditional definition of the increment() function

```
function increment() {
  count.value++;   // One accesses the value of count using
                   count.value
}
```

one can also write the following:

Function increment() defined using ES6 syntax

```
const increment = () => {
  count.value++;
};
```

Now that we know how to define methods in a component, let's explore how to define and use new reactive variables that depend on those already created. These new reactive variables are called computed properties.

Defining Computed Properties in a Vue. js Component

Computed properties allow the creation of new reactive variables based on those already defined. Since computed properties are also reactive, they will be updated if any of the reactive variables they depend on is modified.

The advantage of computed properties is that their result is calculated only if one of the reactive variables associated with them is modified. This saves processing time compared to calling a traditional method (as a method performs its processing each time it is used).

To illustrate this, let's create a new reactive variable named doubleCount, which is used to calculate double the value of the reactive variable count. The variable doubleCount is a computed property because it depends on one or more reactive variables. Its value will be automatically updated whenever any of the reactive variables it depends on is updated.

To define and use a computed property with the Composition API, we use the computed(callback) method defined in Vue.js. The callback() function should return the value of the computed property. The return value of the computed() method is associated with the name of the computed property, in the form of const doubleCount = computed(callback) to create the computed property doubleCount.

Creation of the computed property doubleCount (file src/components/MyCounter.vue)

```
<script setup>
import { ref, computed } from "vue";

// Usage of ref() to create a reactive variable
const count = ref(0);

// Usage of computed() to create a computed variable
const doubleCount = computed(function() {
  return count.value * 2;
});

const increment = () => {
  count.value++;
};

</script>

<template>
```

```
<h3>MyCounter Component</h3>
Reactive variable count: <b>{{ count }}</b>
<br />
Computed variable doubleCount : <b>{{ doubleCount }}</b>
<br /><br />
<button @click="increment()">count+1</button>

</template>
```

After several clicks on the "count+1" button:

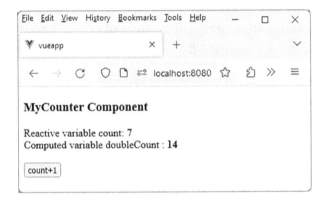

Figure 1-25. *Creation of the computed property doubleCount*

We have seen how to use the click on a button to increment the reactive variable count. But suppose we want to increment the variable automatically, every second, as soon as the component is displayed. We will need to use a new concept, which is to use the lifecycle methods of a Vue.js component.

Lifecycle in a Vue.js Component

When a Vue.js component is created in memory, it follows an internal lifecycle that corresponds to the different phases of its evolution:

1. It is created in memory and then attached to the
    DOM tree of the current HTML page.

2. Next, it is possibly updated, if necessary (in the
    Virtual DOM and then in the real DOM).

3. Finally, it is possibly removed, if necessary (from the
    Virtual DOM and the real DOM).

Each of the preceding steps is associated with an internal method
in the Vue.js component. These internal methods are called lifecycle
methods, and it is possible to use them in each Vue.js component. You can
then write specific processing in each method.

Here are the different lifecycle methods that can be used in a Vue.js
component. They all use a `callback` parameter, which is a function that
describes the processing to be performed when the lifecycle method is
triggered. These methods are executed by Vue.js in the order they are
written here:

1. `setup`: The setup is not associated with a method
    but corresponds to the code written in the `<script
    setup>` section. It is executed only once during the
    creation of the component in memory.

2. `onMounted(callback)`: This method is executed
    only once when the component has been inserted
    into the HTML page. The HTML elements
    associated with the component are in the DOM.

3. `onUpdated(callback)`: This method is executed
    when the component has been updated (in memory
    and in the DOM). It is executed with each update.

4. `onUnmounted(callback)`: This method is executed
    only once when the component is removed
    from memory.

The aforementioned methods allow processing after the insertion, update, or destruction of the component. Other methods exist to perform processing before it is realized. These are the following methods:

1. onBeforeMount(callback): This method is executed only once before the component is inserted into the HTML page.

2. onBeforeUpdate(callback): This method is executed before the component is updated, with each update.

3. onBeforeUnmount(callback): This method is executed only once before the component is removed.

Let's write these methods in the MyCounter component and use them to display traces in the console.

Using lifecycle methods (file src/components/MyCounter.vue)

```
<script setup>
import { ref, computed, onBeforeMount, onMounted,
onBeforeUpdate, onUpdated, onBeforeUnmount, onUnmounted }
from "vue";

console.log("setup: The component is created in memory.");

// Usage of ref() to create a reactive variable
const count = ref(0);

// Usage of computed() to create a computed variable
const doubleCount = computed(function() {
  return count.value * 2;
});
```

```
const increment = () => {
  count.value++;
};

// Lifecycle Methods
onBeforeMount(() => {
  console.log("onBeforeMount: The component is about to be
  mounted in the DOM.");
});

onMounted(() => {
  console.log("onMounted: The component has been mounted in
  the DOM.");
});

onBeforeUpdate(() => {
  console.log("onBeforeUpdate: The component is about to be
  updated.");
});

onUpdated(() => {
  console.log("onUpdated: The component has been updated.");
});

onBeforeUnmount(() => {
  console.log("onBeforeUnmount: The component is about to be
  unmounted.");
});

onUnmounted(() => {
  console.log("onUnmounted: The component has been
  unmounted.");
});
```

```
</script>

<template>

<h3>MyCounter Component</h3>
Reactive variable count: <b>{{ count }}</b>
<br />
Computed variable doubleCount : <b>{{ doubleCount }}</b>
<br /><br />
<button @click="increment()">count+1</button>

</template>
```

Let's run the previous program and observe the traces displayed in the console:

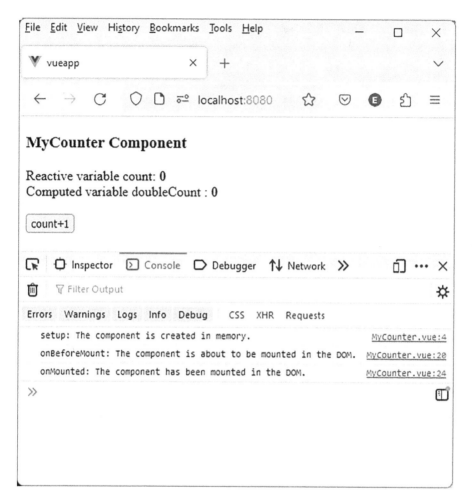

Figure 1-26. *Lifecycle methods*

We can see that the component is first created in memory and then mounted in the DOM.

Let's click the "count+1" button. This will update the component by incrementing the reactive variable count:

Figure 1-27. *Component updated*

The onBeforeUpdate() and onUpdated() methods were executed during the update of the reactive variable.

If we click again the "count+1" button, these methods are executed again:

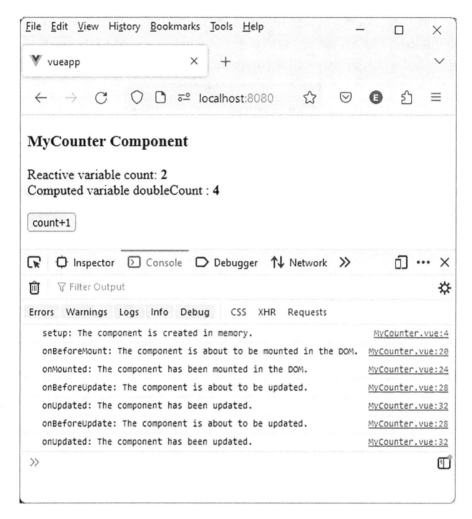

Figure 1-28. *New update of the component*

Example of Using Lifecycle Methods in a Vue.js Component

We've seen when the lifecycle methods are triggered.

Let's see how to use these lifecycle methods so that the MyCounter component displays a counter that increments every second (instead of using the button click as before). To achieve this, we need to use a timer with the setInterval() method of JavaScript. The timer will start in one of the methods indicating the creation of the component (e.g., the onMounted() method), and it will be stopped in one of the methods indicating the removal of the component (e.g., the onUnmounted() method).

We define two new methods in the MyCounter component, which are the start() and stop() methods:

1. The start() method starts the timer and will be called in the onMounted() method.

2. The stop() method stops the timer and will be called in the onUnmounted() method.

Start the counter automatically (file src/components/MyCounter.vue)

```
<script setup>
import { ref, computed, onMounted, onUnmounted } from "vue";

let timer;

const count = ref(0);

const doubleCount = computed(() => count.value * 2);

const increment = () => {
  count.value++;
};

const start = () => {
  timer = setInterval(function() {
    increment();
```

```
  }, 1000);
};

const stop = () => {
  clearInterval(timer);
};

onMounted(() => {
  start();
});

onUnmounted(() => {
  stop();
});

</script>

<template>
<h3>MyCounter Component</h3>
Reactive variable count: <b>{{ count }}</b>
<br />
Computed variable doubleCount : <b>{{ doubleCount }}</b>

</template>
```

Since the counter is started automatically, the "count+1" button has been removed from the component. The start() method is called in the onMounted() method but could have been called directly from the <script setup> section. Let's verify that the counter is now automatically started without having to click the button:

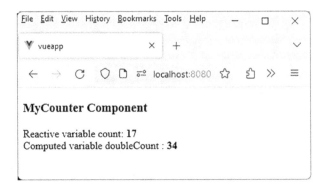

Figure 1-29. *Automatic start of the counter*

The counter is now automatically started when the component is displayed.

Managing Reactivity Ourselves with the customRef( ) Method

In everything we have previously explained, we have seen that whenever a reactive variable is updated, its new value is automatically reflected in the component where it is displayed. This operation is due to the internal functioning of reactivity in Vue.js, which performs it for us. Most of the time, this is the desired behavior.

However, it is possible to create our own reactivity. This would allow us to perform processing before a reactive variable is displayed or before a reactive variable is modified.

Here are some examples of using this mechanism:

- **Date Formatting:** Before displaying a date, we format it according to the format of the country using it. The date would be stored internally in the YYYYMMDD format but would be displayed, for example, in the DD/MM/YYYY format for better display comfort or according to the MM-DD-YYYY format.

- **Email Validation:** Once the email is entered, we check that it is in the correct format before storing it.

- **Processing During Field Entry:** Instead of performing processing for each character entered, we wait for a minimum number of characters to be entered before performing it. This prevents making requests to a server too quickly.

- **Checking the Format of a Password:** It is sometimes useful to check that the chosen password has characteristics such as at least ten characters, at least one digit, at least one uppercase letter, at least one lowercase letter, etc.

This operation is possible, thanks to the customRef() method, which allows creating reactive variables with a specific behavior. Let's now examine how the customRef() method works to define new reactive variables.

Step 1: Operation and Use of customRef( )

A reactive variable defined with customRef() works in the same way as one defined with ref(). Thus, the value property of the variable allows accessing it in both reading and writing.

However, we define ourselves what the reading of the variable should return and also what the variable should finally contain when its value is initialized or modified. This is the advantage of using this type of reactive variables defined by customRef() rather than ref(), as we can modify the result of reading and/or the result of writing the variable, and this in a centralized manner (in the customRef() method).

The difference with the `ref()` method is that reading a variable defined with `ref()` returns the exact value of the content of the variable, and its writing writes exactly into the variable what is indicated in the value attribute.

The questions to ask when creating a variable with `customRef()` are as follows:

- What do we want to get back when reading the variable?

- What do we want to get in the content of the variable when it is modified?

If the answer to these two questions is to keep the current value, just use the `ref()` method to create the reactive variable. The `customRef()` method would not add anything more in this case.

The `customRef(callback)` method uses the `callback(track, trigger)` function, which allows returning an object with the properties { `get, set` }, which are functions defining the reading of the variable (with the `get()` function) and the modification of the variable (with the `set()` function).

- The `get()` function must return the value we want to read when accessing the variable (in reading).

- The `set(newValue)` function must set the new value of the variable (in writing). The `newValue` parameter is the value we want to write, but it can be modified in the `set()` method.

The `track()` and `trigger()` parameters of the callback function are functions to call when you want to trigger reading (by `track()`) or update (by `trigger()`).

To understand these explanations, the simplest way is to write a minimal program that does this work. The traces written in the program will help understand how it works.

We create a count variable defined by customRef(), which increments by 1 with each click on a "count+1" button.

Incrementing a count variable defined by customRef() (file src/components/MyCounter.vue)

```
<script setup>
import { customRef } from 'vue';

// Create a custom reference (customRef)
const count = customRef((track, trigger) => {
  let value = 0;  // value will be the variable being tracked,
  initialized here to 0.
  return {
    get() {
      // Track the dependency when the value is read.
      track();
      console.log("get value =", value);
      return value;
    },
    set(newValue) {
      // Update the value and trigger reactivity.
      value = newValue;
      trigger();
      console.log("set value =", value);
    }
  };
});

function increment() {
  console.log("before increment value");
  count.value += 1;  // Increment the value of the variable.
  console.log("after increment value");
}
```

```
</script>

<template>

<h3> MyCounter Component </H3>

Reactive variable count: <b>{{ count }}</b>
<br><br>
<button @click="increment">count + 1</button>

</template>
```

The count variable is created when calling the customRef(callback) method. Once the count variable is created, it can be used by writing instructions like count.value += 1, which here increments the value by 1. The usage principle is the same as if the variable had been created by ref().

The callback function used in customRef(callback) has the form callback(track, trigger), where track() will be used in the get() method and trigger() in the set() method.

The callback function starts by creating a variable (here value) that will be the internally manipulated variable and corresponds to the value of the count variable. The variable is initialized to 0 here.

The callback function then returns an object { get, set } that defines the get() and set() methods:

- The get() method calls the track() method, indicating that we want to track the variable mentioned next, and its value is returned by get().

- Here, we want to return the exact value of the variable that will be used when reading the count variable, but we could return something else.

- The set(newValue) method calls the trigger()
  method to indicate that we are going to modify the
  variable's value, and this new value must be taken into
  account. Here, we assign the newValue to value, but we
  could assign another value.

The implemented functionality here corresponds to the functionality used with the ref() method. However, it allows, with the traces performed in the methods, to see the internal functioning provided by the customRef() method.

Let's execute the previous program, displaying the traces in the console (F12 key):

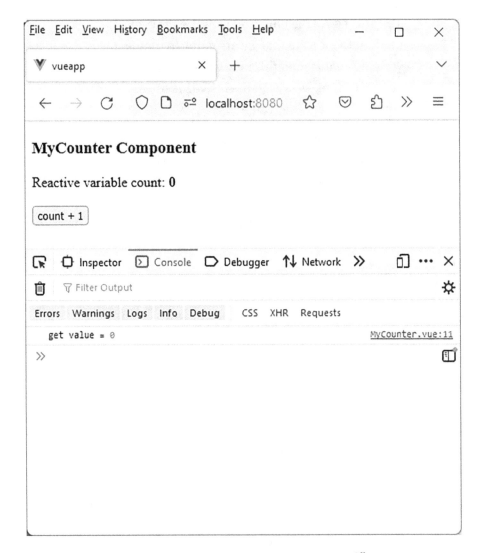

Figure 1-30. *Using a variable defined by customRef()*

We can see that at the program's launch, the get() method is called to retrieve the variable's value and display it in the component.

Next, let's click the "count+1" button.

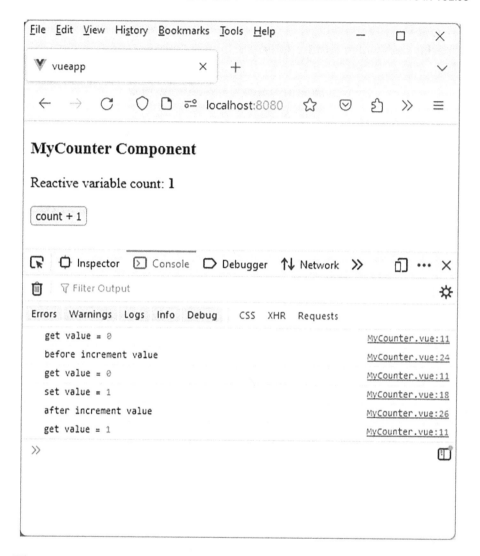

Figure 1-31. *Incrementing a variable defined by customRef()*

When clicking the "count+1" button, the click handling function `increment()` is executed. We can see in the traces that to execute the `count.value += 1;` instruction, we first read the value (via `get()`) and then update the value (via set()). Afterward, a final read (via get()) is performed, which corresponds to displaying the new value in the component.

Now that we have seen the internal functioning of customRef(), let's use it to produce more interesting results.

Step 2: Limiting the Increment of a Variable

During the variable update (in the set() method), it is possible to decide the value that will finally be assigned to the variable.

For example, we can create a counter that stops at the value 10 without being able to exceed it.

For this example, we use a "count+1" button that increments the counter and a "count - 1" button that decrements it. Once the maximum value is reached, we can only decrement the counter, which can then be incremented again.

Using a maximum value (file src/components/MyCounter.vue)

```
<script setup>
import { customRef } from 'vue';

// Maximum value not to be exceeded
const maximum = 10;

// Create a custom reference (customRef)
const count = customRef((track, trigger) => {
  let value = 0;  // value will be the variable being tracked,
                  initialized here to 0.

  return {
    get() {
      // Track the dependency when the value is read.
      track();
```

```
      return value;
    },
    set(newValue) {
      // Update the value and trigger reactivity.
      if (newValue <= maximum) value = newValue;
      trigger();
    }
  };
});

function increment() {
  count.value += 1;   // Increment the value of the variable.
}

function decrement() {
  count.value -= 1;   // Decrement the value of the variable.
}

</script>

<template>

<h3> MyCounter Component </H3>

Reactive variable count: <b>{{ count }}</b>
<br><br>
Maximum: <b>{{ maximum }}</b>
<br><br>
<button @click="increment">count + 1</button>
 
<button @click="decrement">count - 1</button>

</template>
```

We use a variable named `maximum` with a value of 10. Since this variable will not be modified, there is no need to make it reactive. The `count` variable is managed by `customRef()`. The value of the variable managed by `customRef()` is modified only if it is less than the maximum value. When the maximum value (here, 10) is reached, the counter is locked:

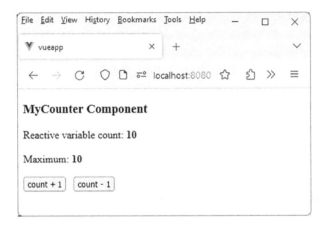

Figure 1-32. *Blocking the counter at the maximum value*

We have prevented the possibility of incrementing the value of the count variable. Let's delve further into program structuring by creating a function known as a "composable" that easily creates reactive variables with the characteristic of limiting their value to a maximum.

Step 3: Create a Composable useMaximum( ) to Limit the Value

Instead of creating the `count` variable by defining it in the component's code, we create a function that generates the desired variable. This allows us to reuse the function in various parts of the program if necessary.

This approach will be explored in Chapter 6 and corresponds to the creation of composables. Composables are utility functions that can be used elsewhere in the program or even in other projects.

Here, we will create the useMaximum() composable, which limits the value of the reactive variable to the specified max value.

Create and use the useMaximum(max) composable (file src/components/MyCounter.vue)

```
<script setup>
import { customRef } from 'vue';

// Maximum value not to be exceeded
const maximum = 10;

const useMaximum = (max) => {
  // Create a custom reference (customRef)
  return customRef((track, trigger) => {
    let value = 0;  // value will be the variable being
    tracked, initialized here to 0.
    return {
      get() {
        // Track the dependency when the value is read.
        track();
        return value;
      },
      set(newValue) {
        // Update the value and trigger reactivity.
        if (newValue <= max) value = newValue;
        trigger();
      }
    };
  });
}
```

```
const count = useMaximum(maximum);

function increment() {
  count.value += 1;   // Increment the value of the variable.
}

function decrement() {
  count.value -= 1;   // Decrement the value of the variable.
}

</script>

<template>

<h3> MyCounter Component </H3>

Reactive variable count: <b>{{ count }}</b>
<br><br>
Maximum: <b>{{ maximum }}</b>
<br><br>
<button @click="increment">count + 1</button>
 
<button @click="decrement">count - 1</button>

</template>
```

The count variable is now created when calling the useMaximum() method. This approach allows us to easily create multiple variables of this type.

It is customary for the composable to be placed in a separate file. Therefore, we create the file useMaximum.js, which corresponds to the source code of the useMaximum() composable. This file is placed in the src/composables directory, which is created if necessary.

Composable useMaximum() (file src/composables/useMaximum.js)

```
import { customRef } from "vue";

const useMaximum = (max) => {
  // Create a custom reference (customRef)
  return customRef((track, trigger) => {
    let value = 0;   // value will be the variable being
                     tracked, initialized here to 0.

    return {
      get() {
        // Track the dependency when the value is read.
        track();
        return value;
      },
      set(newValue) {
        // Update the value and trigger reactivity.
        if (newValue <= max) value = newValue;
        trigger();
      }
    };
  });
}

export default useMaximum;
```

The code of the MyCounter component can then be simplified. It is enough to import the composable useMaximum() file into the component:

MyCounter component using the useMaximum() composable (file src/components/MyCounter.vue)

```
<script setup>

import useMaximum from "../composables/useMaximum.js"
```

```
// Maximum value not to be exceeded
const maximum = 10;

const count = useMaximum(maximum);

function increment() {
  count.value += 1;  // Increment the value of the variable.
}

function decrement() {
  count.value -= 1;  // Decrement the value of the variable.
}

</script>

<template>

<h3> MyCounter Component </H3>

Reactive variable count: <b>{{ count }}</b>
<br><br>
Maximum: <b>{{ maximum }}</b>
<br><br>
<button @click="increment">count + 1</button>
 
<button @click="decrement">count - 1</button>

</template>
```

The component's code is simplified. The functionality remains the same.

Step 4: Create a Composable useFormatDate( ) to Format Dates

A final example of using customRef() would be to create a composable that displays dates according to the desired format:

- MM-DD-YYYY (internal format "en-US")

- DD-MM-YYYY (internal format "en-GB")

- MM/DD/YYYY (internal format "en-US")

- DD/MM/YYYY (internal format "en-GB")

The useFormatDate() composable returns a reactive variable with the desired format.

Composable useFormatDate(date, format) (file src/components/ MyCounter.vue)

```
<script setup>
import { customRef } from "vue";

const formatDate = (date, format) => {
  const options = { year: 'numeric', month: '2-digit',
  day: '2-digit' };

  if (format == "MM-DD-YYYY")
    return date.toLocaleDateString('en-US', options).
    replace(/\//g, '-');
  else if (format == "DD-MM-YYYY")
    return date.toLocaleDateString('en-GB', options).
    replace(/\//g, '-');
  else if (format == "MM/DD/YYYY")
    return date.toLocaleDateString('en-US', options);
  else if (format == "DD/MM/YYYY")
```

```
    return date.toLocaleDateString('en-GB', options);
}
const useFormatDate = (date, format) => {
  return customRef((track, trigger) => {
    let value = date;  // value will be the tracked variable
    return {
      get() {
        // track the dependency when the value is read
        track();
        return formatDate(value, format);
      },
      set(newValue) {
        // update the value and trigger reactivity
        value = newValue;
        trigger();
      }
    };
  });
};

const date= new Date();   // Current date

const dateMMDDYYYY = useFormatDate(date, "MM-DD-YYYY");
const dateDDMMYYYY = useFormatDate(date, "DD-MM-YYYY");
const dateMMDDYYYY_slash = useFormatDate(date, "MM/DD/YYYY");
const dateDDMMYYYY_slash = useFormatDate(date, "DD/MM/YYYY");

</script>

<template>

<h3> MyCounter Component </H3>
```

```
<hr>
Current date : {{date}}
<hr>
Date (MM-DD-YYYY) : <b>{{ dateMMDDYYYY }}</b>
<br><br>
Date (DD-MM-YYYY) : <b>{{ dateDDMMYYYY }}</b>
<br><br>
Date (MM/DD/YYYY) : <b>{{ dateMMDDYYYY_slash }}</b>
<br><br>
Date (DD/M/YYYY) : <b>{{ dateDDMMYYYY_slash }}</b>
<br><br>

</template>
```

We display today's date in various formats. The obtained result is displayed as follows:

Figure 1-33. *Displaying dates in various formats*

As in the previous example, it is desirable to create a separate file that contains the code for the composable. This simplifies the component's writing and enables the use of the composable in other components.

The file for the useFormatDate() composable will be registered in a file named useFormatDate.js, located in the src/composables directory.

Composable useFormatDate() (file src/composables/ useFormatDate.js)

```
import { customRef } from "vue";

const formatDate = (date, format) => {
  const options = { year: 'numeric', month: '2-digit', day:
  '2-digit' };

  if (format == "MM-DD-YYYY")
    return date.toLocaleDateString('en-US', options).
    replace(/\//g, '-');
  else if (format == "DD-MM-YYYY")
    return date.toLocaleDateString('en-GB', options).
    replace(/\//g, '-');
  else if (format == "MM/DD/YYYY")
    return date.toLocaleDateString('en-US', options);
  else if (format == "DD/MM/YYYY")
    return date.toLocaleDateString('en-GB', options);
}

const useFormatDate = (date, format) => {
  return customRef((track, trigger) => {
    let value = date;  // value will be the tracked variable
    return {
      get() {
        // track the dependency when the value is read
        track();
```

```
      return formatDate(value, format);
    },
    set(newValue) {
      // update the value and trigger reactivity
      value = newValue;
      trigger();
    }
  };
});
};

export default useFormatDate;
```

The code for the MyCounter component becomes the following:

MyCounter component using the useFormatDate() composable (file src/components/MyCounter.vue)

```
<script setup>
```

import useFormatDate from "../composables/useFormatDate.js"

```
const date= new Date();   // Current date

const dateMMDDYYYY = useFormatDate(date, "MM-DD-YYYY");
const dateDDMMYYYY = useFormatDate(date, "DD-MM-YYYY");
const dateMMDDYYYY_slash = useFormatDate(date, "MM/DD/YYYY");
const dateDDMMYYYY_slash = useFormatDate(date, "DD/MM/YYYY");

</script>

<template>

<h3> MyCounter Component </H3>

<hr>
Current date : {{date}}
```

```
<hr>
Date (MM-DD-YYYY) : <b>{{ dateMMDDYYYY }}</b>
<br><br>
Date (DD-MM-YYYY) : <b>{{ dateDDMMYYYY }}</b>
<br><br>
Date (MM/DD/YYYY) : <b>{{ dateMMDDYYYY_slash }}</b>
<br><br>
Date (DD/M/YYYY) : <b>{{ dateDDMMYYYY_slash }}</b>
<br><br>

</template>
```

Step 5: Entering Text in Uppercase

Another use of this mechanism is, for example, to enter text in uppercase, which standardizes the entry of names in an application. The field is transformed into uppercase as characters are entered into the field.

We still use the MyCounter component in which a variable named name corresponding to an input field is displayed. To achieve this, we use the v-model directive, which will be explained in the next chapter.

The input in the field is displayed in uppercase letters, regardless of the entered letters.

Entering text in uppercase (file src/components/MyCounter.vue)

```
<script setup>
import { customRef } from 'vue';

const name = customRef((track, trigger) => {
  let value = "";  // value will be the tracked variable
  return {
    get() {
      // track the dependency when the value is read
```

```
      track();
      return value.toUpperCase();
    },
    set(newValue) {
      // update the value and trigger reactivity
      value = newValue;
      trigger();
    }
  };
});
```

```
</script>

<template>

<h3> MyCounter Component </H3>

<b>Uppercase Input:</b>
<br><br>
Variable name: <input type="text" v-model="name" />
<br><br>
Variable name: {{ name }}

</template>
```

As explained earlier, it is sufficient to replace the value to be read from the variable with its uppercase representation. This is done in the get() method.

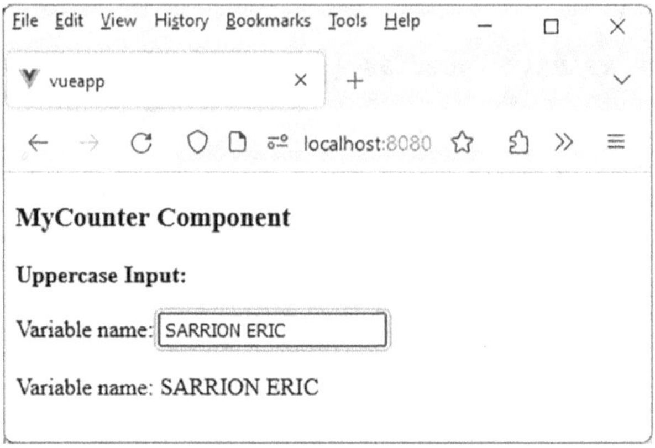

Figure 1-34. *Uppercase name input*

It is also possible to create a separate file that defines the useUpperCase(initialValue) composable with an initialValue parameter. The file useUpperCase.js will be placed in the src/ composables directory.

Composable useUpperCase(initialValue) (file src/composables/ useUpperCase.js)

```
import { customRef } from 'vue';

const useUpperCase = (initValue) => {
  return customRef((track, trigger) => {
    let value = initValue;   // value will be the tracked
                             variable

    return {
      get() {
        // track the dependency when the value is read
        track();
        return value.toUpperCase();
      },
      set(newValue) {
```

```
        // update the value and trigger reactivity
        value = newValue;
        trigger();
      }
    };
  });
};
```

```
export default useUpperCase;
```

The use of the useUpperCase() composable in the MyCounter component is as follows:

MyCounter component using the useUpperCase() composable (file src/components/MyCounter.vue)

```
<script setup>
```

```
import useUpperCase from "../composables/useUpperCase.js"
```

```
const name = useUpperCase("eric");
```

```
</script>
```

```
<template>
```

```
<h3> MyCounter Component </H3>
```

```
<b>Uppercase Input:</b>
<br><br>
Variable name: <input type="text" v-model="name" />
<br><br>
Variable name: {{ name }}
```

```
</template>
```

The component is initialized with the variable name set to the value "eric", which will be immediately displayed in uppercase in both the input field and the following text.

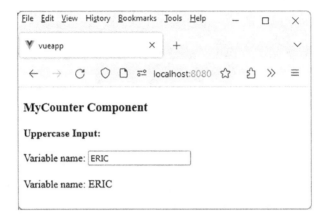

Figure 1-35. *Utilization of the useUpperCase() composable*

Conclusion

We have come a long way during this first day dedicated to mastering Vue.js! We have covered the necessary steps for creating the first Vue.js application, from installing Vue.js to analyzing the generated files.

We have also delved into key concepts such as component structuring, reactivity, defining methods and computed properties, as well as managing the lifecycle of components.

In the upcoming chapters, we will further deepen our Vue.js skills and explore more advanced concepts to create high-performance web applications. So get ready for the exciting continuation of this learning journey!

CHAPTER 2

Day 2: Mastering Directives in Vue.js

In this chapter, we will delve into directives in Vue.js, a key element for mastering this front-end library. Directives allow us to add new functionalities to HTML elements on the page.

We will explore several essential directives, such as `v-bind`, `v-if`, `v-else`, `v-show`, and `v-for`, providing detailed steps to understand how they function.

Next, we will focus on the `v-model` directive, which is particularly useful for two-way data binding in forms.

Finally, we will address the use of modifiers in Vue.js, which allow us to modify the behavior of directives.

Using Attributes in Vue.js Components

A component is similar to an HTML element and can have attributes (also called props, meaning properties).

Let's use two new attributes, named `init` and `end`, in the `MyCounter` component:

- The `init` attribute indicates the initialization value of the counter. If this attribute is not specified, its starting value is considered as 0.

- The end attribute indicates the final value of the counter. If this attribute is not specified, the counter does not stop.

As long as the counter value (incremented every second) is between the init and end values, the counter continues to increment. Once the end value is reached (if specified in the attributes), the counter stops.

Step 1: Using the init and end Attributes in the MyCounter Component

An example of using the MyCounter component with the init and end attributes could be the following:

Counter from 10 to 20

```
<MyCounter init="10" end="20" />
```

If the attribute values are written, as shown previously, within quotes (in the form of strings, "10" and "20"), they are string literals passed to the MyCounter component. To use the attribute value as a numeric value in the MyCounter component, it will employ the JavaScript function parseInt(value), which returns the numeric representation of the value if it wasn't already numeric. We will demonstrate how to write the content of the MyCounter component in the following section.

Alternatively, one can use the MyCounter component in the following form, without representing the attributes as strings:

Counter from 10 to 20

```
<MyCounter init=10 end=20 />
```

In this case, the numeric values 10 and 20 are passed to the MyCounter component. To indicate a counter that starts at 10 but never stops, the end attribute is omitted in the MyCounter component's definition:

Counter from 10 to infinity

```
< MyCounter init=10 />
```

Finally, to indicate a counter that counts from 0 to infinity, no attributes are specified in the MyCounter component:

Counter from 0 to infinity

```
< MyCounter />
```

It is also possible to set the value of an attribute based on the value of a variable initialized in the program. For example, if we define the variable init initialized to the value 10, we can write in the src/App.vue file:

Counter initialized from the init variable (file src/App.vue)

```
<script setup>

import MyCounter from './components/MyCounter.vue'

const init = 10;  // The variable init is equal to 10

</script>

<template>

<MyCounter :init="init" />

</template>

<style scoped>
</style>
```

The init variable is defined in the <script> section of the component. It is accessible in the <template> section of the component by writing :init="init". The syntax :init="init" signifies that the init attribute (indicated as :init) is initialized with the value of the init variable (indicated as "init").

The ":" symbol before an attribute name indicates to interpret the following value as a JavaScript expression. One could also write `<MyCounter :init="init+3" />` to start the counter with the value 13 instead of 10, as `"init+3"` is a valid JavaScript expression.

The quotes around the value of the JavaScript expression are necessary if the JavaScript expression contains spaces. Thus, writing `="init"` or `=init` are equivalent expressions.

To initialize the counter with the numeric value 10, one can also write the following:

Initialize the init attribute to the numeric value 10

```
<MyCounter :init="10" />
```

Indeed, specifying `:init` instead of just `init` for the attribute name indicates that the following value is a JavaScript expression, specifically the numeric value 10 and not the string "10".

We have seen how to write and use the `MyCounter` component in various forms with the `init` and `end` attributes. Let's now explore how the `MyCounter` component is written to make use of these attributes.

Step 2: Writing the MyCounter Component That Utilizes the init and end Attributes

The code associated with the `MyCounter` component must consider the various possible forms for writing the attributes.

The attributes will be defined in the `<script setup>` section of the component, using Vue.js's `defineProps()` method.

MyCounter component with init and end attributes (file src/components/MyCounter.vue)

```
<script setup>
import { ref, computed, onMounted, onUnmounted, defineProps }
from 'vue';

let timer;

const props = defineProps(["init", "end"]);
// Declaration of the "init" and "end" attributes

const init = props.init || 0;    // 0: default value
const end = props.end || 0;  // 0: default value

const count = ref(parseInt(init));
const doubleCount = computed(() => count.value * 2);

const increment = () => {
  if (!end || count.value < parseInt(end)) count.value++;
  else stop();
};

const start = () => {
  timer = setInterval(() => {
    increment();
  }, 1000);
};

const stop = () => {
  clearInterval(timer);
};

onMounted(() => {
  start();
});
```

```
onUnmounted(() => {
  stop();
});
```

```
</script>
```

```
<template>
  <h3>MyCounter Component</h3>
  init : {{init}} => end : {{end}}
  <br /><br />
  Reactive variable count : <b>{{ count }}</b>
  <br />
  Computed variable doubleCount : <b>{{ doubleCount }}</b>
</template>
```

The defineProps() method is used by specifying, in an array, the name of each attribute.

When retrieving the value of the attribute by writing const init = props.init, it is mandatory to provide a default value for the attribute (here, 0, by writing props.init || 0). Otherwise, the retrieval into a variable cannot be performed. In such a case, one would be forced to use the init attribute in the form props.init throughout the program, which would not be convenient.

The values of the attributes, retrieved into the variables init and end, are then displayed in the template using {{init}} and {{end}}.

For example, suppose the MyCounter component is used as follows:

Counter from 10 to 20 (file src/App.vue)

```
<script setup>
```

```
import MyCounter from "./components/MyCounter.vue"
```

```
</script>
```

```
<template>
```

`<MyCounter init=10 end=20 />`

```
</template>
```

The counter starts at the value 10 and ends at the value 20. Let's run
the program:

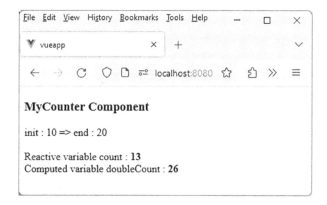

Figure 2-1. *Using the init and end attributes*

The counter starts from the value 10 and will stop when it reaches the
value 20.

Passing an Object As Attributes

Instead of passing the init and end attributes individually to the
MyCounter component, these values can also be transmitted within a
JavaScript object.

Let's call the new attribute limits, which will replace the init and
end attributes. The limits attribute will take the form {init: 10, end:
20}. Let's demonstrate how to use this attribute within the MyCounter
component.

The App component, which uses the MyCounter component, is modified as follows:

App component using the MyCounter component and its limits attribute (file src/App.vue)

```
<script setup>

import MyCounter from "./components/MyCounter.vue"

</script>

<template>

<MyCounter :limits="{init:10, end:20}" />

</template>
```

The value of the limits attribute is specified as an object {init: 10, end: 20}. Adding a string around the object is optional if the following value does not contain spaces (here, the string is required because there is a space before the end attribute).

To ensure that Vue.js interprets the specified value as a JavaScript value (here, an object), it must be indicated by writing the attribute as :limits rather than just limits.

Let's see how the code of the MyCounter component is modified to accommodate the new limits attribute.

MyCounter component using the limits attribute (file src/components/ MyCounter.vue)

```
<script setup>
import { ref, computed, onMounted, onUnmounted, defineProps }
from 'vue';

let timer;

const props = defineProps(["limits"]);
```

```
const init = props.limits.init || 0;
const end = props.limits.end || 0;

const count = ref(parseInt(init));
const doubleCount = computed(() => count.value * 2);

const increment = () => {
  if (!end || count.value < parseInt(end)) count.value++;
  else stop();
};

const start = () => {
  timer = setInterval(() => {
    increment();
  }, 1000);
};

const stop = () => {
  clearInterval(timer);
};

onMounted(() => {
  start();
});

onUnmounted(() => {
  stop();
});

</script>

<template>
  <h3>MyCounter Component</h3>
  init : {{init}} => end : {{end}}
  <br /><br />
```

```
Reactive variable count : <b>{{ count }}</b>
<br />
Computed variable doubleCount : <b>{{ doubleCount }}</b>
</template>
```

The limits attribute is defined in the defineProps() method as
["limits"]. The init value is retrieved from props.limits.init, and
the end value is retrieved from props.limits.end. When the end value is
reached, the counter stops:

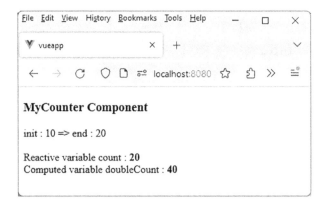

Figure 2-2. *Using the limits attribute*

We have seen how to define attributes for Vue.js components. Vue.js
also allows the use of another form of attributes called directives. These
are powerful tools. Let's now explore how to use the standard directives
provided by Vue.js. In Chapter 5, we will learn how to create our own
directives, extending Vue.js's capabilities.

Differences Between Directives and Attributes in Vue.js

A Vue.js directive is used similarly to an attribute. What then is the difference between the two?

1. An attribute represents a static value, information transmitted to the component or HTML element on which it is positioned. In the previous examples, we used the `init` and `end` attributes to statically indicate the starting and ending values of the counter. The same applies to HTML attributes associated with HTML elements. For example, the `class` attribute allows specifying a CSS class for the HTML element on which it is positioned.

2. On the other hand, Vue.js directives are used to add dynamic logic to an HTML element or Vue.js component, reacting to changes in data or performing specific actions in response to events. Directives allow binding HTML elements to the state of the Vue.js application, making the user interface responsive and interactive based on application data and logic.

A simple example of a Vue.js directive, which will be explained in the following, is the `v-show` directive. It is used in the form `v-show="condition"`. This directive shows or hides the element on which it is positioned based on the value specified in the condition. If the condition evaluates to `true`, the element is displayed; otherwise, it is hidden. This demonstrates the dynamic aspect of the directive, as opposed to static attributes.

To differentiate Vue.js directives from regular attributes (HTML attributes or those created in our components, such as the init and end attributes mentioned earlier), Vue.js directives all start with the prefix "v-". Examples include v-if, v-show, v-bind, v-on, etc., which we will explain in the following.

Let's start with the v-bind directive.

v-bind Directive

The v-bind directive allows using attribute values that will be reactive, similar to reactive variables used in HTML.

For example, let's use the previous counter, where the value increments upon clicking the "count+1" button. Suppose we want to display the counter value in an input field. For this, we would like to write something like <input type="text" value="{{count}}" />. Indeed, it is hoped that, thanks to the reactivity of the count variable, the value of the input field will be updated when the counter is incremented.

Let's write this in the template of the MyCounter component. The MyCounter component becomes as follows:

Display the count variable in the value attribute of an input field (file src/components/MyCounter.vue)

```
<script setup>

import { ref, computed } from "vue"

const count = ref(0);
const doubleCount = computed(() => count.value * 2);

const increment = () => {
  count.value++;
};

</script>
```

```
<template>

  <h3>MyCounter Component</h3>
  Reactive variable count : <b>{{ count }}</b>
  <br />
  Computed variable doubleCount : <b>{{ doubleCount }}</b>
  <br/>
  Input : <input type="text" value="{{count}}" />
  <br/><br/>

  <button @click="increment()">count+1</button>

</template>
```

The App component that displays the MyCounter component is as follows:

App component (file src/App.vue)

```
<script setup>

import MyCounter from "./components/MyCounter.vue"

</script>

<template>

<MyCounter />

</template>
```

After several clicks on the "count+1" button, the displayed result is as follows:

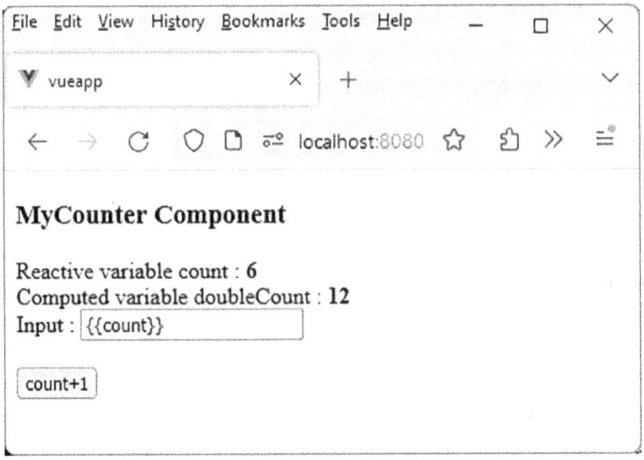

Figure 2-3. *Reactive variable in the value attribute*

The counter increments, but the value displayed in the input field does not reflect this change.

The use of {{count}} in the value attribute does not update the content of the input field, which remains fixed with the string "{{count}}". To initialize and update the value attribute of the input field with the value of the reactive variable count, a directive called v-bind must be used. The v-bind directive allows binding the value of an attribute to that of a reactive variable.

Therefore, one would write <input type="text" v-bind:value="count" />, which binds the value attribute of the input field to the value of a reactive variable, in this case, the count variable.

The template of the MyCounter component becomes the following:

Display the count variable in the value attribute of an input field (file src/components/MyCounter.vue)

```
<script setup>

import { ref, computed } from "vue"

const count = ref(0);
const doubleCount = computed(() => count.value * 2);
```

```
const increment = () => {
  count.value++;
};

</script>

<template>

  <h3>MyCounter Component</h3>
  Reactive variable count : <b>{{ count }}</b>
  <br />
  Computed variable doubleCount : <b>{{ doubleCount }}</b>
  <br/>
  Input : <input type="text" v-bind:value="count" />
  <br/><br/>

  <button @click="increment()">count+1</button>

</template>
```

Now, we obtain correct initialization and updates of the input field based on the changes in the reactive variable count.

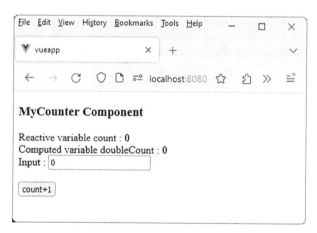

Figure 2-4. *Reactive variable in the value attribute with the v-bind directive*

The input field is now initialized with the value of the reactive variable count, which is 0.

As the count variable is reactive, incrementing it causes the update of its display wherever it is used, including in the input field.

Let's click the "count+1" button several times:

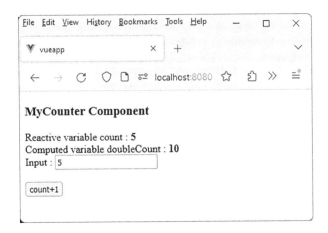

Figure 2-5. *Modification of the reactive variable count*

The value displayed in the input field is updated to reflect the value of the reactive variable count.

The v-bind directive is commonly used in templates. For this reason, Vue.js allows simplifying the syntax by writing :value="count" instead of v-bind:value="count".

We had already used this simplified form of the v-bind directive by writing :init="10" or :init="init" in the previous pages.

One could also write v-bind:value="count+3" because the value "count+3" is a JavaScript expression interpreted by v-bind.

Additionally, one can write the shorthand form :value="count+3", which is equivalent to v-bind:value="count+3".

Refreshing a Component by Modifying Its Attributes

The following example demonstrates how to update a component by transmitting new values to its attributes.

In this scenario, we want the "count+1" button to be integrated into the App component rather than the MyCounter component. This means that the App component should handle the incrementation of the counter and transmit this counter value to the MyCounter component through attributes. With each increment of the counter value in the App component, the MyCounter component refreshes to display the new value.

The App component becomes as follows:

App component (file src/App.vue)

```
<script setup>

import { ref, computed } from 'vue';
import MyCounter from './components/MyCounter.vue';

const count = ref(0);
const doubleCount = computed(()=>count.value*2);
const increment = () => {
  count.value++;
};

</script>

<template>
  <MyCounter :count="count" :doubleCount="doubleCount" />
  <br /><br />
  <button @click="increment()">count+1</button>
</template>
```

The logic for incrementing the counter is implemented in the App component. The counter values (count and doubleCount) are transmitted in the attributes of the MyCounter component, which then displays them. The MyCounter component is refreshed each time one of its attributes is modified.

Step 1: Using Attributes in the <template> Section of the MyCounter Component

The MyCounter component, which utilizes the transmitted attributes, becomes as follows:

MyCounter component (file src/components/MyCounter.vue)

```
<script setup>

import { defineProps } from "vue"

// Enabling access to the attributes count and doubleCount in
the template
defineProps(["count", "doubleCount"]);

</script>

<template>

  <h3>MyCounter Component</h3>
  Reactive variable count : <b>{{ count }}</b>
  <br />
  Computed variable doubleCount : <b>{{ doubleCount }}</b>
  <br/>
  Input : <input type="text" v-bind:value="count" />

</template>
```

The defineProps(["count", "doubleCount"]) method identifies the attributes count and doubleCount, which will then be directly used by their names in the <template> section.

Note that the props variable typically returned by defineProps() is unnecessary here. It would be useful if you wanted to use the attribute values in the <script setup> section.

Let's verify that everything is working:

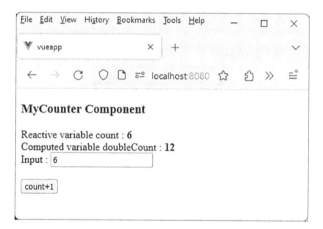

Figure 2-6. *Updating the counter through its attributes*

Step 2: Using Attributes in th <script setup> Section of the MyCounter Component

If you want to use the transmitted count and doubleCount attributes in the <script setup> section of the MyCounter component, you need to access them directly using the props variable, in the form of props.count and props.doubleCount. The variables count and doubleCount, corresponding to the attributes, can only be used under these names in the <template> section.

Let's use props.count in the <script setup> section. As this value is updated with each increment, we display its value in the onUpdated() lifecycle method.

Using props.count in <script setup> (file src/components/MyCounter.vue)

```
<script setup>

import { defineProps, onUpdated } from "vue"

const props = defineProps(["count", "doubleCount"]);

console.log("setup : count = ", props.count);

onUpdated(() => {
  console.log("updated : count = ", props.count);
})

</script>

<template>

  <h3>MyCounter Component</h3>
  Reactive variable count : <b>{{ count }}</b>
  <br />
  Computed variable doubleCount : <b>{{ doubleCount }}</b>
  <br/>
  Input : <input type="text" v-bind:value="count" />

</template>
```

We display the value of props.count in the <script setup> section of the component (creation) and then with each update in the onUpdated() method.

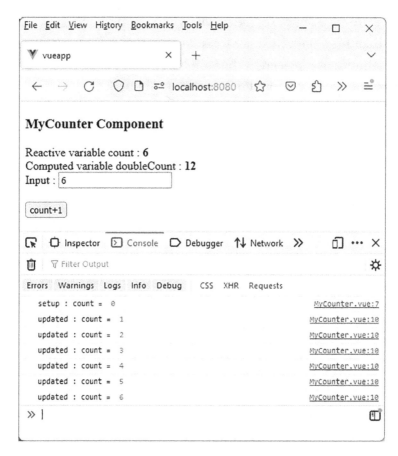

Figure 2-7. *Using attributes in <script setup>*

Through this example, we can observe that updating at least one of the attributes of a component refreshes the entire component.

v-if and v-else Directives

The v-if and v-else directives make it easy to write conditional tests in a component's template.

Let's use the example of the previous counter, adding a Start button to start the counter. Once the counter is started by clicking the Start button, the Start button is replaced by the Stop button, which allows stopping the counter. Therefore, the counter is started or stopped (depending on its state) by alternately clicking on the displayed Start or Stop button.

The v-if and v-else directives will allow us to alternately display the Start button or the Stop button:

- The v-if directive is used by specifying a JavaScript expression that represents a boolean value. If the value of the expression is true, the element using this directive is inserted into the page; otherwise, it is not.

- The v-else directive is used on the following element (at the same level). The element using the v-else directive will be inserted into the page if the one using v-if is not.

If the v-else directive is used, it must follow an element with a v-if directive.

In the following, the App component is restored to its initial state:

App component (file src/App.vue)

```
<script setup>

import MyCounter from './components/MyCounter.vue'

</script>

<template>

<MyCounter />

</template>
```

Let's now write the MyCounter component, which alternately displays the Start and Stop buttons. We will first code it in an intuitive way, but it won't work. Then, we'll see the modifications needed to achieve the desired result.

Step 1: Writing the MyCounter Component in an Intuitive (but Nonfunctional…) Way

Based on what we have previously explained, it would be natural to code the MyCounter component as follows:

MyCounter component with alternated Start and Stop buttons (file src/components/MyCounter.vue)

```
<script setup>
import { ref, computed } from "vue"
let timer = null;
const count = ref(0);
const doubleCount = computed(() => count.value * 2);

const increment = () => {
  count.value++;
};

const start= () => {
  timer = setInterval(() => increment(), 1000);
}

const stop = () => {
  clearInterval(timer);
  timer = null;
}

</script>
```

```
<template>

  <h3>MyCounter Component</h3>
  Reactive variable count : <b>{{ count }}</b>
  <br />
  Computed variable doubleCount : <b>{{ doubleCount }}</b>
  <br /><br />
  <button v-if="!timer" @click="start()">Start</button>
  <button v-else @click="stop()">Stop</button>

</template>
```

The interesting part is the one written with the v-if and v-else directives:

- The v-if directive displays the Start button if the value of the timer variable is null, which is the case when the HTML page is initially displayed because the timer variable is initialized to null.

- The v-else directive displays the Stop button if the timer variable has a different value (i.e., not null).

This code looks logical and functional. Let's try to see the result obtained.

When the program is launched, the counter is at 0, and the Start button is displayed. This corresponds to the executed v-if directive.

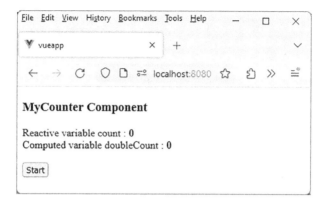

Figure 2-8. *Start button displayed*

Let's click the Start button. The counter starts, and the Stop button is displayed:

Figure 2-9. *The counter has started*

The Stop button is displayed, corresponding to the execution of the v-else directive. Everything seems to be working.

Let's click the Stop button to stop the counter:

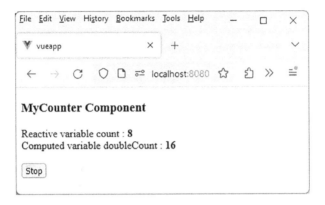

Figure 2-10. *The counter has been stopped*

Clicking the Stop button has stopped the counter. However, the button label is still "Stop" when it should be "Start." Additionally, clicking the button again does not restart the counter, which remains stuck at the stopped value.

So there is an issue. Let's explain why and resolve it now.

Step 2: Writing the MyCounter Component After Corrections (And Functional!)

The frequently made mistake is using a nonreactive variable in a directive, as seen with the `timer` variable, which is not reactive but is used in the `v-if` directive. Since the `timer` variable is not reactive, its modification is not considered by the `v-if` directive, which observes changes only on reactive variables.

We simply need to transform the `timer` variable into a reactive variable and modify the code where it is used, using `timer.value` instead of just `timer`.

**The timer variable is defined as reactive (file src/components/
MyCounter.vue)**

```
<script setup>

import { ref, computed } from "vue"

const timer = ref(null);
const count = ref(0);
const doubleCount = computed(() => count.value * 2);

const increment = () => {
  count.value++;
};

const start= () => {
  timer.value = setInterval(() => increment(), 1000);
}

const stop = () => {
  clearInterval(timer.value);
  timer.value = null;
}

</script>

<template>

  <h3>MyCounter Component</h3>
  Reactive variable count : <b>{{ count }}</b>
  <br />
  Computed variable doubleCount : <b>{{ doubleCount }}</b>
  <br /><br />
  <button v-if="!timer" @click="start()">Start</button>
  <button v-else @click="stop()">Stop</button>

</template>
```

111

After stopping the counter, the Start button is now visible, and the counter can restart:

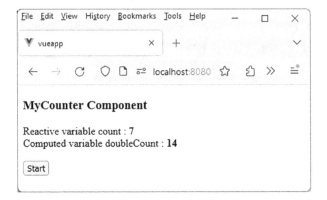

Figure 2-11. *The counter can restart*

Clicking the Start button restarts the counter:

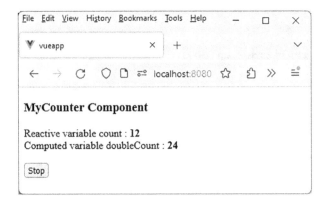

Figure 2-12. *The counter has restarted*

v-show Directive

The v-show directive is similar to the v-if directive. The difference is that v-if inserts the element into the page if the condition specified in the directive is true whereas v-show inserts it in all cases but only displays it if the condition is true (the v-show directive uses the element's style to hide or show it as needed).

Using the v-show directive in the previous template, we write the following:

Using the v-show directive (file src/components/MyCounter.vue)

```
<template>

  <h3>MyCounter Component</h3>
  Reactive variable count : <b>{{ count }}</b>
  <br />
  Computed variable doubleCount : <b>{{ doubleCount }}</b>
  <br /><br />
  <button v-show="!timer" @click="start()">Start</button>
  <button v-show="timer" @click="stop()">Stop</button>

</template>
```

The v-show directive, being used with a condition, requires writing the negation of the first condition in the second v-show directive. Using v-if and v-else avoids writing two conditions (only one condition will be written in the v-if directive).

The result obtained is the same as the previous one.

v-for Directive

The v-for directive allows for looping, enabling the insertion of the directive-containing element into the HTML page multiple times.

The value of the v-for directive can be written in several ways, depending on the need:

1. **First Form of Writing:** v-for="i in n". This form of writing allows for a loop from 1 to the value n.

2. **Second Form of Writing:** v-for="item, i in items". This form of writing allows for traversing the items array and performing an operation for each element item in the array.

Let's start by studying the writing form v-for="i in n", which allows for a loop from 1 to the value n.

Step 1: v-for Directive in the Form v-for="i in n"

The variable i corresponds to the index in the loop (starting from 1), while the variable n corresponds to the final value of the index in the loop.

To use this form of the v-for directive, suppose we want to display multiple counters like the previous one. We would then have a new MyCounters component that incorporates several MyCounter components using a v-for directive. For example, we would write <MyCounters :nb="3" /> to indicate that we want to display three MyCounter components on the page. The nb attribute indicates how many MyCounter components we want to display in the HTML page.

The App component is modified to display the MyCounters component:

App component displaying the MyCounters component (file src/ App.vue)

```
<script setup>

import MyCounters from "./components/MyCounters.vue"

</script>

<template>

<MyCounters :nb="3" />

</template>
```

Notice that if we specify :nb="3" instead of nb="3", it allows us to transmit the numeric value 3 to the MyCounters component rather than the string "3". Indeed, if an attribute is preceded by the ":" sign, it means that we should interpret the following value (in quotes or not) as a JavaScript expression.

The MyCounters component uses the v-for directive to display the MyCounter components:

MyCounters component (file src/components/MyCounters.vue)

```
<script setup>

import MyCounter from "./MyCounter.vue";
import { defineProps } from 'vue';

defineProps(["nb"]);

</script>

<template>

<MyCounter v-for="i in nb" />

</template>
```

The v-for directive placed on an element allows displaying that element as many times as indicated in the value of the directive (here, from 1 to the value of the nb variable).

The MyCounter component is the same as before:

MyCounter component (file src/components/MyCounter.vue)

```
<script setup>

import { ref, computed } from "vue"

const timer = ref(null);
const count = ref(0);
const doubleCount = computed(() => count.value * 2);

const increment = () => {
  count.value++;
};

const start= () => {
  timer.value = setInterval(() => increment(), 1000);
}

const stop = () => {
  clearInterval(timer.value);
  timer.value = null;
}

</script>

<template>

  <h3>MyCounter Component</h3>
  Reactive variable count : <b>{{ count }}</b>
  <br />
  Computed variable doubleCount : <b>{{ doubleCount }}</b>
```

```
<br /><br />
<button v-if="!timer" @click="start()">Start</button>
<button v-else @click="stop()">Stop</button>
```

```
</template>
```

Let's look at the result obtained:

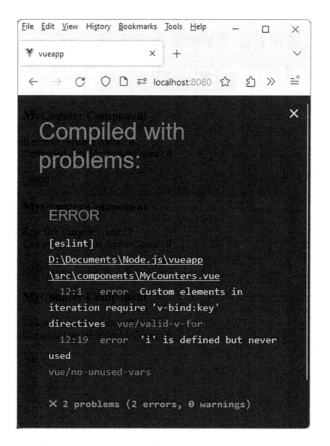

Figure 2-13. *Misuse of the v-for directive*

We encounter two errors:

1. It is necessary to use the v-bind:key directive when using the v-for directive.

2. The variable i used in the v-for="i in nb"
directive is defined but not used.

These errors are quite common when starting to develop Vue.js applications. We explain how to resolve these errors in the following section. It is sufficient to use an attribute named key in the v-for directive.

Step 2: Use the Key Attribute with the v-for Directive

The previous error shows that the use of the v-for directive must be accompanied by the use of the v-bind:key directive. This v-bind:key directive allows defining a special attribute reserved for Vue.js (key attribute) that provides a unique key to each repetitively inserted element.

The key attribute is an attribute used internally by Vue.js and cannot be used by us in the component on which it is positioned.

To resolve the previous error, it is sufficient to specify a key attribute with the value of the variable i. As the variable i varies from 1 to nb, the key attribute of each inserted MyCounter component will thus have a different value, which is what we want.

By using the key attribute in this way, we solve both of the previous errors at the same time.

Use of the key attribute (file src/components/MyCounters.vue)

```
<script setup>

import MyCounter from "./MyCounter.vue";
import { defineProps } from 'vue';

defineProps(["nb"]);

</script>
```

```
<template>
```

`<MyCounter v-for="i in nb" v-bind:key="i" />`

```
</template>
```

The `v-bind:key="i"` directive can be simplified by simply writing `:key="i"`. We had explained this writing simplification previously when using the `v-bind` directive.

Now we have the following:

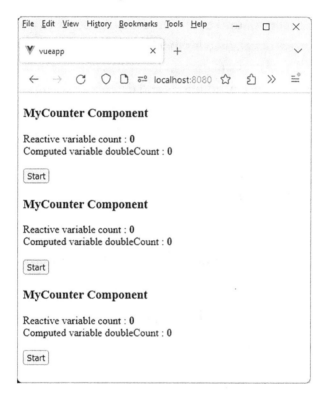

Figure 2-14. *Display of three counters in the MyCounters component*

Step 3: Rules Regarding the Key Attribute

The key attribute is mandatory when using a v-for directive, regardless of the form of the directive. Here are two rules regarding this attribute:

1. The value of the key attribute must be unique in the list.

2. And this value should never be modified (in the case where the list is updated).

Indeed, if a value of the key attribute is assigned to a list item, this value must always be retained for that item. Vue.js uses this value to determine if a list item is still present in the list, in order to refresh the list correctly (in the case of additions and deletions of items in the list). Therefore, if, as in our previous example, the index of the list item is used in the key attribute, it will only work if the list is static (as is the case in our example).

To build dynamic lists, it is generally recommended to use a unique ID identifier associated with each list item.

Step 4: Use an Index in the Component That Uses v-for

Suppose we want to number the previous counters, here from 1 to 3. The key attribute contains this value from 1 to 3 but cannot be used directly in the component because it is prohibited by Vue.js and produces an error. The key attribute is indeed for internal use by Vue.js.

To remedy this, simply create a new attribute, named, for example, index, which will have the same value. The index attribute can be used directly in the MyCounter component.

The MyCounters component is modified to set the index attribute following the v-for directive:

Index attribute positioned following the v-for directive (file src/ components/MyCounters.vue)

```
<script setup>

import MyCounter from "./MyCounter.vue";
import { defineProps } from 'vue';

defineProps(["nb"]);

</script>

<template>
```

<MyCounter v-for="i in nb" :key="i" :index="i" />

```
</template>
```

The index attribute is positioned on the MyCounter component following the v-for directive. Its value will be that of the variable i and will thus be 1, then 2, and finally 3.

The index attribute is usable within the MyCounter component. It is sufficient to retrieve this attribute using the defineProps(["index"]) method.

Note that if you write defineProps(["key"]), this will result in an error, as explained earlier.

Usage of the index attribute in the MyCounter component (file src/ components/MyCounter.vue)

```
<script setup>

import { ref, computed, defineProps } from "vue"

const timer = ref(null);
const count = ref(0);
const doubleCount = computed(() => count.value * 2);
```

```
defineProps(["index"]);

const increment = () => {
  count.value++;
};

const start= () => {
  timer.value = setInterval(() => increment(), 1000);
}

const stop = () => {
  clearInterval(timer.value);
  timer.value = null;
}

</script>

<template>

  <h3> {{index}} - MyCounter Component </h3>
  Reactive variable count : <b>{{ count }}</b>
  <br />
  Computed variable doubleCount : <b>{{ doubleCount }}</b>
  <br /><br />
  <button v-if="!timer" @click="start()">Start</button>
  <button v-else @click="stop()">Stop</button>

</template>
```

The counters are now numbered:

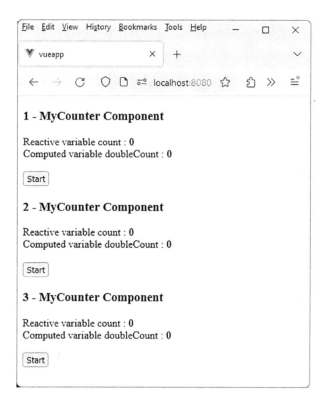

Figure 2-15. *Numbering of counters*

The counters are now numbered starting from 1. Of course, each counter starts and stops independently. For example, let's start the second counter:

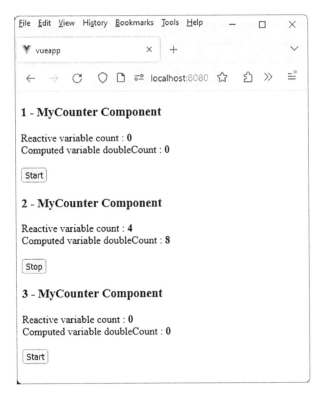

Figure 2-16. *Counter 2 started*

We have previously seen how to use the `v-for` directive in the form `v-for="i in n"`, which allows looping from 1 to n. Now, let's explore how to loop through an array of elements using another form of the `v-for` directive, namely, `v-for="(item, i) in items"`.

Step 5: v-for Directive in the Form v-for="(item, i) in items"

The second form of the v-for directive enables looping through an array of elements represented by the variable items. Each element in the array is represented by the variable item. The variable i corresponds to the index of the element in the array, starting from 0 (unlike the previous form of the directive where it started from 1).

It is possible to omit the parentheses and write the directive as v-for="item, i in items" and also as v-for="item in items" if the index i is not being used.

Let's assume the variable items is an array indicating, for each counter, the starting value (init property) and the end value of that counter (end property). In the following component code, the variable items is referred to as limits:

The App component is as follows:

App component (file src/App.vue)

```
<script setup>

import MyCounters from './components/MyCounters.vue'

const limits = [
  {init: 0, end: 10},
  {init: 5},
  {end: 10}
];

</script>

<template>

<MyCounters :limits="limits" />

</template>
```

125

The `limits` array is an array of objects `{ init, end }`, indicating for each counter its initial value (`init`) and final value (`end`):

- If the initial value `init` is not specified, it is considered to be 0.

- If the final value `end` is not specified, it is considered infinite (the counter has no end limit).

The `App` component incorporates the `MyCounters` component in the form of `<MyCounters :limits="limits" />`. This way, the `limits` array is passed to the `MyCounters` component as the `limits` attribute, which will be utilized within the component.

The `MyCounters` component displays `MyCounter` components based on the content of the `limits` array:

MyCounters component (file src/components/MyCounters.vue)

```
<script setup>

import MyCounter from "./MyCounter.vue";
import { defineProps } from 'vue';
```

defineProps(["limits"]);

```
</script>

<template>
```

<MyCounter v-for="(limit, i) in limits" :key="i" :index="i" :limit="limit" />

```
</template>
```

The `MyCounter` component receives the attributes `index` and `limit`:

- The `index` attribute represents the index of the element in the list, starting from 0.

- The limit attribute corresponds to an object { init, end }, as defined in the limits array.

The MyCounter component is slightly modified to display the init and end parameters it receives through the limit attribute. If an initial value (init) is not transmitted, it is displayed as 0. If a final value (end) is not transmitted, "infinity" is displayed.

MyCounter component (file src/components/MyCounter.vue)

```
<script setup>
import { ref, computed, defineProps } from "vue"

const props = defineProps(["limit", "index"]);
const init = props.limit.init || 0;          // 0 if no init
                                             indicated
const end = props.limit.end || undefined;    // undefined if no
                                             end indicated
const timer = ref(null);
const count = ref(init);
const doubleCount = computed(() => count.value * 2);

const increment = () => {
  if (end == undefined || count.value < end) count.value++;
};

const start= () => {
  timer.value = setInterval(() => increment(), 1000);
}

const stop = () => {
  clearInterval(timer.value);
  timer.value = null;
}

</script>
```

```
<template>

  <h3> {{index}} - MyCounter Component </h3>
  init = {{init}}, end = {{end ? end : "infinity"}}
  <br />
  Reactive variable count : <b>{{ count }}</b>
  <br />
  Computed variable doubleCount : <b>{{ doubleCount }}</b>
  <br /><br />
  <button v-if="!timer" @click="start()">Start</button>
  <button v-else @click="stop()">Stop</button>

</template>
```

The three counters are displayed here:

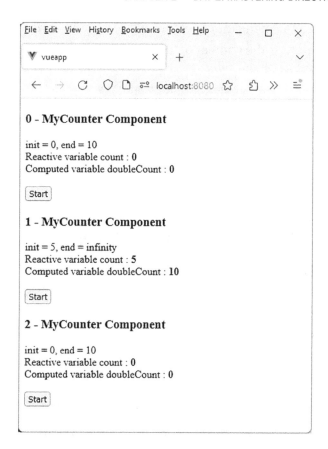

Figure 2-17. *Counters with displayed init and end attributes*

Each counter now has the init and end attributes displayed, retrieved from the limit attribute of the MyCounter component.

v-model Directive

The v-bind directive we studied earlier allows updating an attribute associated with a reactive variable when that variable is modified. For example, the instruction <input v-bind:value="count" /> updates the `value` attribute of the input field when the reactive variable `count` is changed. Therefore, the content of the input field is automatically updated.

Conversely, modifying the `value` attribute of the input field does not update the associated reactive variable `count`. To achieve this, the `v-model` directive is used.

The `v-model` directive enables two-way binding (attribute to variable and variable to attribute), while the `v-bind` directive allows modification in only one direction (variable to attribute).

Step 1: Difference Between v-bind and v-model Directives

To observe the behavioral difference between the `v-bind` and `v-model` directives, let's use the `MyCounter` component, which displays the reactive variable `count` and two input fields:

- The first input field is managed by `v-bind`.

- The second input field is managed by `v-model`.

The `MyCounter` component is directly inserted into the `App` component:

App component (file src/App.vue)

```
<script setup>

import MyCounter from './components/MyCounter.vue'

</script>

<template>

<MyCounter />

</template>
```

The MyCounter component becomes the following:

MyCounter component (file src/components/MyCounter.vue)

```
<script setup>
import { ref, computed } from "vue"

const count = ref(0);
const doubleCount = computed(() => count.value * 2);

</script>

<template>

  <h3> MyCounter Component </h3>
  Reactive variable count : <b>{{ count }}</b>
  <br />
  Computed variable doubleCount : <b>{{ doubleCount }}</b>
  <br /><br />
  Input for count (using v-bind): <input type="text"
  :value="count" />
  <br/><br/>
  Input for count (using v-model): <input type="text"
  v-model="count" />

</template>
```

Indeed, to use the v-bind directive, you can simplify the syntax by writing :value="count" instead of v-bind:value="count". During program execution, the value of the reactive variable (here, 0) initializes the content of both input fields. This is achieved through the functionality of the v-bind directive, and it's worth noting that the v-model directive also incorporates the behavior of v-bind.

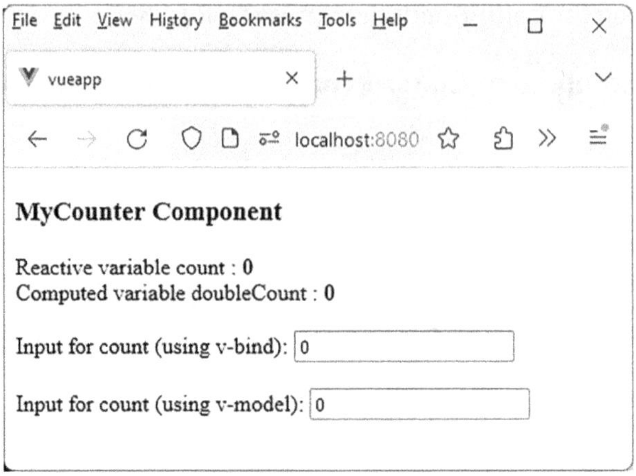

Figure 2-18. *Initialization of input fields (v-bind operation)*

The distinction between the v-bind and v-model directives becomes apparent when modifying the values in the input fields. If you modify the first input field using the v-bind directive, the reactive variable count does not get updated:

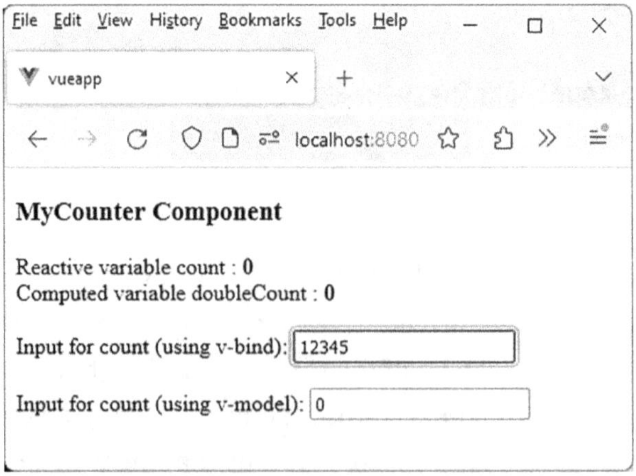

Figure 2-19. *Modification of the input field using v-bind*

Indeed, an attribute managed by the v-bind directive is updated if the associated reactive variable is modified, but not vice versa. Therefore, modifying the value attribute of the input field does not alter the associated reactive variable count.

On the other hand, if you modify the second input field using the v-model directive, the reactive variable count updates (thanks to v-model), leading to the modification of the first input field using v-bind (due to the behavior of the v-bind directive).

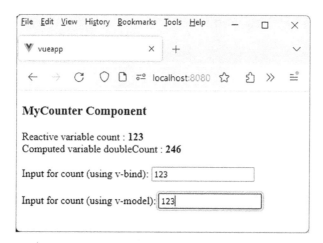

Figure 2-20. *Modification of the input field using v-model*

Step 2: Using the v-model Directive in Forms

We have seen the usefulness of the v-model directive in managing an input field, automatically capturing the content of the input field in a reactive variable.

The v-model directive is widely employed in input forms to easily retrieve the values entered/checked/selected in the form. Each form field is simply connected to a reactive variable using the v-model directive.

Let's use the `v-model` directive to retrieve and display information entered in a form, allowing the input of information displayed in various forms:

- An input field for the person's name

- A selection list to choose the year of birth

- Radio buttons to choose marital status

- Finally, check boxes to validate terms of use and general sales conditions

Figure 2-21. *Input form managed by v-model*

The advantage of using the v-model directive with the fields in this form is that modifying each field immediately updates the reactive variable associated with that field. The values of the reactive variables associated with each field are displayed below the form.

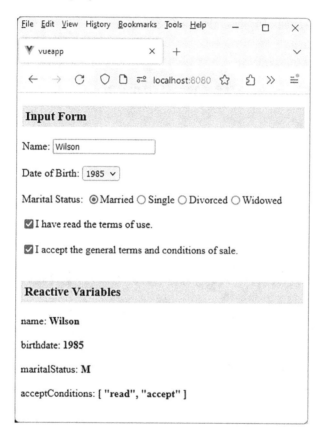

Figure 2-22. *Reactive variables updated according to input*

The fact that each form field is linked to a reactive variable through v-model allows for retrieving the current input or selection in the form. Let's explore how to manage each form field based on its type (input field, selection list, radio buttons, or check boxes).

A new component called MyForm is used, which will contain the previous display. The component file MyForm.vue is created in the src/ components directory. The MyForm component is inserted into the App component:

App component using the MyForm component (file src/App.vue)

```
<script setup>

import MyForm from "./components/MyForm.vue"

</script>

<template>

<MyForm />

</template>
```

Step 3: Managing Input Fields with v-model

This case is the one we previously studied, which served as an introduction to the v-model directive. The MyForm component becomes the following:

Input field in the MyForm component (file src/components/ MyForm.vue)

```
<script setup>
import { ref } from "vue"
const name = ref("");
</script>
<template>
<h3>Input Form</h3>
Name: <input type="text" v-model="name" />
```

```
<br/><br/>

<h3>Reactive Variables</h3>
name: <b>{{name}}</b>
<br/><br/>

</template>

<style scoped>
h3 {
  background-color: gainsboro;
  padding: 5px;
}
</style>
```

After entering data into the field, you get:

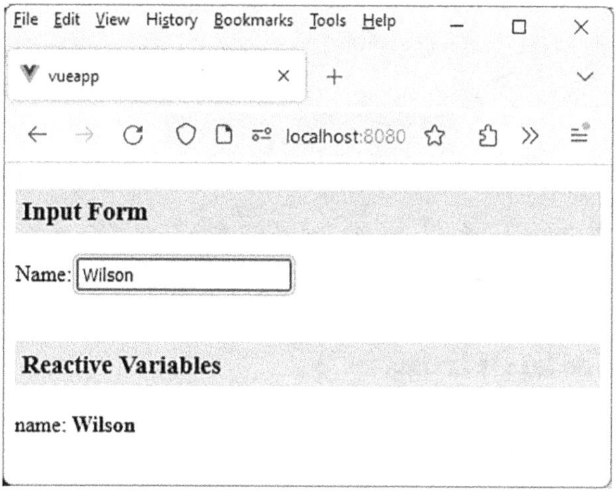

Figure 2-23. *Entering the name in the form*

Step 4: Managing Selection Lists with v-model

Now, let's see how to retrieve the selected value in a list, for example, the year of birth.

Selection list in the MyForm component (file src/components/ MyForm.vue)

```
<script setup>

import { ref } from "vue"

const name = ref("");
let dates = [];
for (let year=2023; year > 1900; year--) dates.push(year);
const birthdate = ref("");

</script>

<template>

<h3>Input Form</h3>
Name: <input type="text" v-model="name" />
<br/><br/>
Date of Birth:
  <select v-model="birthdate" >
    <option v-for="date in dates" :value="date"
    :key="date">{{date}}</option>
  </select>
<br/><br/>

<h3>Reactive Variables</h3>
name: <b>{{name}}</b>
<br/><br/>
birthdate: <b>{{birthdate}}</b>
```

```
<br/><br/>

</template>

<style scoped>
h3 {
  background-color: gainsboro;
  padding: 5px;
}
</style>
```

The v-model directive is used on the <select> element. Each year in the list is displayed using a v-for directive, iterating over "date in dates". The dates array has been previously populated in the <script setup> section of the component. If a date is chosen from the list, the selected date is displayed in the reactive variable birthdate:

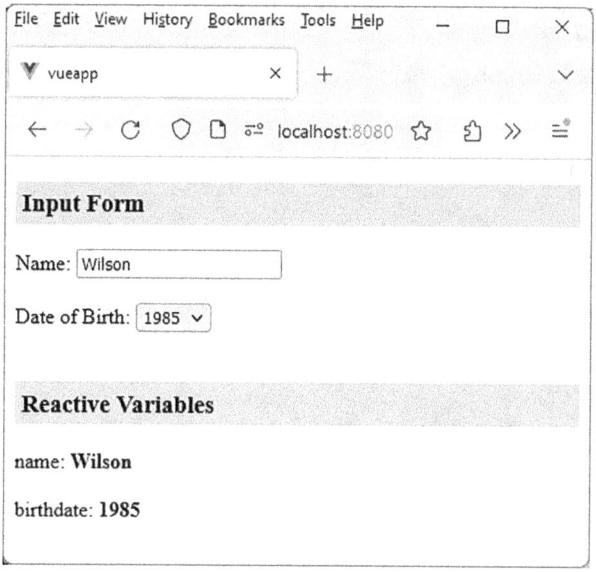

Figure 2-24. *Selecting a date in the form*

Step 5: Managing Radio Buttons with v-model

Now, let's see how to retrieve the value of the selected radio button. Here, radio buttons are used to choose marital status: Married, Single, Divorced, Widowed. Only one radio button at a time is selected in the list.

Managing radio buttons in the form (file src/components/ MyForm.vue)

```
<script setup>

import { ref } from "vue"

const name = ref("");
let dates = [];
for (let year=2023; year > 1900; year--) dates.push(year);
const birthdate = ref("");
const maritalStatus = ref("");

</script>

<template>

<h3>Input Form</h3>
Name: <input type="text" v-model="name" />
<br/><br/>
Date of Birth:
  <select v-model="birthdate" >
    <option v-for="date in dates" :value="date" :key="date">
    {{date}}</option>
  </select>
<br/><br/>
Marital Status:
```

```
    <input type="radio" value="M" id="maried"
    v-model="maritalStatus">
    <label for="maried">Married</label>
    <input type="radio" value="S" id="single"
    v-model="maritalStatus">
    <label for="single">Single</label>
    <input type="radio" value="D" id="divorced"
    v-model="maritalStatus">
    <label for="divorced">Divorced</label>
    <input type="radio" value="W" id="widower"
    v-model="maritalStatus">
    <label for="widower">Widowed</label>
<br/><br/>

<h3>Reactive Variables</h3>
name: <b>{{name}}</b>
<br/><br/>
birthdate: <b>{{birthdate}}</b>
<br/><br/>
maritalStatus: <b>{{maritalStatus}}</b>
<br/><br/>

</template>

<style scoped>
h3 {
  background-color: gainsboro;
  padding: 5px;
}
</style>
```

The `v-model` directive is applied to each `<input type="radio">` element. The same reactive variable, `maritalStatus`, is associated with each element.

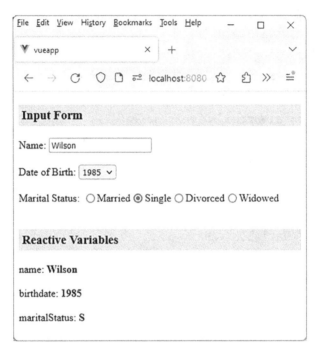

Figure 2-25. *Managing radio buttons in the form*

Step 6: Managing Check Boxes with v-model

Finally, let's see how to handle check boxes in forms. Here, two check boxes are used, which can be checked independently:

- The first one indicates that the terms of use have been read.

- The second one indicates that the general terms and conditions of sale have been accepted.

Managing check boxes in the form (file src/components/MyForm.vue)

```
<script setup>

import { ref } from "vue"

const name = ref("");
let dates = [];
for (let year=2023; year > 1900; year--) dates.push(year);
const birthdate = ref("");
const maritalStatus = ref("");
const acceptConditions = ref([]);

</script>

<template>

<h3>Input Form</h3>
Name: <input type="text" v-model="name" />
<br/><br/>
Date of Birth:
  <select v-model="birthdate" >
    <option v-for="date in dates" :value="date" :key="date">
    {{date}}</option>
  </select>
<br/><br/>
Marital Status:
  <input type="radio" value="M" id="maried"
  v-model="maritalStatus">
  <label for="maried">Married</label>
  <input type="radio" value="S" id="single"
  v-model="maritalStatus">
```

```
  <label for="single">Single</label>
  <input type="radio" value="D" id="divorced"
  v-model="maritalStatus">
  <label for="divorced">Divorced</label>
  <input type="radio" value="W" id="widower"
  v-model="maritalStatus">
  <label for="widower">Widowed</label>
<br/><br/>
<input type="checkbox" id="read" value="read"
          v-model="acceptConditions" />
<label for="read">I have read the terms of use.</label>
<br/><br/>
<input type="checkbox" id="accept" value="accept"
          v-model="acceptConditions" />
<label for="accept">I accept the general terms and conditions
of sale.</label>
<br/><br/>

<h3>Reactive Variables</h3>
name: <b>{{name}}</b>
<br/><br/>
birthdate: <b>{{birthdate}}</b>
<br/><br/>
maritalStatus: <b>{{maritalStatus}}</b>
<br/><br/>
acceptConditions: <b>{{acceptConditions}}</b>
<br/><br/>

</template>

<style scoped>
h3 {
```

```
background-color: gainsboro;
padding: 5px;
}
</style>
```

The reactive variable `acceptConditions`, which can contain the values of two check boxes, is initialized as an empty array [ ]. Depending on which check box is checked, its value will automatically be added to the `acceptConditions` array.

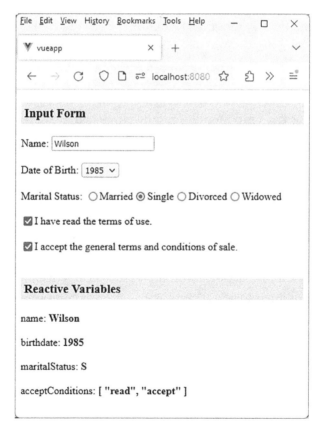

Figure 2-26. *Handling check boxes in the form*

Using Modifiers in Vue.js

Some directives in Vue.js can have what are called modifiers. These modifiers allow modifying the default behavior of the directive.

Take the example of the v-model directive mentioned earlier. It has the following modifiers:

- lazy: The lazy modifier changes the behavior of updating the reactive variable associated with the directive. It updates the variable only when exiting the input field, rather than updating it for every character entered. When the lazy modifier is used, Vue.js considers the change event (for updating the associated reactive variable) instead of the input event.

- trim: The trim modifier removes any leading or trailing spaces from the input field when updating the associated reactive variable.

A modifier is used after the name of the associated directive, prefixed with the "." character. For example, you write v-model.trim="count" or v-model.lazy="count". Additionally, you can combine multiple modifiers by writing v-model.trim.lazy="count".

Let's use the lazy modifier with the v-model directive, taking the name input field from the previous example. The MyForm component is modified to accommodate the lazy modifier in the directive.

Using the lazy modifier (file src/components/MyForm.vue)

```
<script setup>

import { ref } from "vue"

const name = ref("");

</script>
```

```
<template>

<h3>Input Form</h3>
Name: <input type="text" v-model.lazy="name" />
<br/><br/>

<h3>Reactive Variables</h3>
name: <b>{{name}}</b>
<br/><br/>

</template>

<style scoped>
h3 {
  background-color: gainsboro;
  padding: 5px;
}
</style>
```

Let's enter a name in the input field associated with v-model:

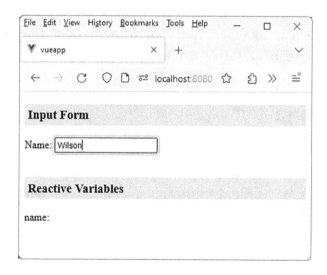

Figure 2-27. *Modifying an input field with the "lazy" modifier*

Now, we can see that the reactive variable no longer updates as we type, contrary to the usual behavior of the v-model directive. However, as soon as we exit the input field, the reactive variable name updates.

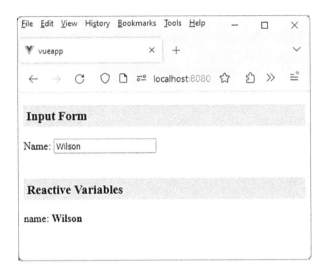

Figure 2-28. *Updating the reactive variable upon exiting the input field*

There are many modifiers available depending on the directives used. It is also possible to create new modifiers (see Chapter 5).

Conclusion

This chapter has provided us with an in-depth understanding of directives in Vue.js, ranging from using attributes to mastering directives like v-bind, v-if, and v-model. These skills are fundamental for building robust and maintainable Vue.js applications.

The next chapter will guide us through handling DOM events, a crucial skill to enhance interactivity in Vue.js applications.

CHAPTER 3

Day 3: Mastering Events in Vue.js

In this third day of our Vue.js study, we will focus on event handling, a crucial element for creating interactive applications with Vue.js.

You will learn how to intercept events related to user actions in the HTML page and use these events to enable components to exchange information. This skill is crucial for increasing the reactivity and interactivity of your Vue.js applications.

Intercepting Events

Vue.js allows you to perform a process when an event occurs using the v-on directive. To specify the event you want to handle, write its name after v-on, preceded by ":". For example, you write v-on:click to indicate that you want to handle the click event.

To handle a click on a button, you write the following:

Activate the increment() method when the button is clicked

```
<button v-on:click="increment()">Increment</button>
```

The value of the v-on directive corresponds to the action to be performed when the event occurs, in this case, calling the increment() function. Since the use of the v-on directive is so common, Vue.js allows

© Eric Sarrion 2024
E. Sarrion, *Master Vue.js in 6 Days*, https://doi.org/10.1007/979-8-8688-0364-2_3

simplifying its syntax by using @click instead of v-on:click. Therefore, you can also write the following:

Activate the increment() method when the button is clicked

```
<button @click="increment()">Increment</button>
```

An example handling a click on a button in the MyCounter component to increment a reactive variable would be as follows:

App Component (file src/App.vue)

```
<script setup>

import MyCounter from "./components/MyCounter.vue"

</script>

<template>

<MyCounter />

</template>
```

The file for the MyCounter component is as follows:

MyCounter Component (file src/components/MyCounter.vue)

```
<script setup>

import { ref } from "vue"

const count = ref(0);

const increment = () => {
  count.value++;
}

</script>

<template>
```

```
<h3>MyCounter Component</h3>
Reactive variable count : <b>{{count}}</b>
<br/><br/>
<button v-on:click="increment()">count+1</button>

</template>
```

After several clicks on the button, the reactive variable count has been incremented:

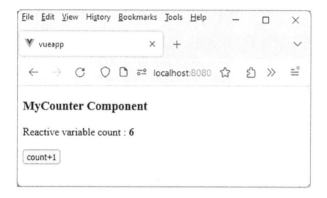

Figure 3-1. *Handling click on the button*

Writing in the Form "increment( )" or "increment"?

When writing the event handling function, you can use either @click="increment()" or simply @click="increment".

Writing in the form "increment()" allows for specifying potential parameters, such as the increment value. You would then write @click="increment(2)" to increment by 2 with each click. The increment function with a parameter would look like this:

MyCounter Component (file src/components/MyCounter.vue)

```
<script setup>
```

```
import { ref } from "vue"

const count = ref(0);
const increment = (value) => {
  count.value += value;
}

</script>

<template>

<h3>MyCounter Component</h3>
Reactive variable count : <b>{{count}}</b>
<br/><br/>
<button v-on:click="increment(2)">count+1</button>

</template>
```

Each click increments the counter by 2 instead of 1.

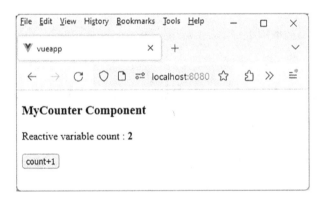

Figure 3-2. *Incrementing by 2 instead of 1*

Therefore, in cases where you want to indicate a parameter, you write it as `"increment(2)"`. In other cases, you can write `"increment()"` or `"increment"` interchangeably.

Using the Event Object

Sometimes it's useful for the event-handling function to know the parameters of that event. For example:

- For a mouse click, which mouse button was used, and the coordinates of the mouse pointer at the click

- For a keyboard press, which key was pressed

This information is available by using the event object (handled by Vue.js) in the event-handling function. The event object is available in all Vue.js event-handling functions.

Let's see a few examples of how to use the event object in event-handling functions.

Step 1: Filtering Pressed Keys

Here's a first example. Let's use the event object to filter allowed keys in an input field, allowing only digits from 0 to 9 and keys for moving or modifying the field.

We will use the keydown event for this purpose. The keydown event is generated with each keystroke before the key is processed and displayed in the input field. The keyup event is triggered after the key is processed, preventing the filtering of allowed keys if used here.

Therefore, we write the MyCounter component as follows:

Filtering keyboard keys (file src/components/MyCounter.vue)

```
<script setup>

import { ref } from "vue"

const count = ref();
```

153

```
const verifyKey = () => {
  const numbers = ["0", "1", "2", "3", "4", "5", "6", "7",
  "8", "9"];
  const moves = ["Backspace", "ArrowLeft", "ArrowRight",
                 "Delete", "Tab", "Home", "End"];

  let authorized;  // Allowed keys in the input field
                   authorized = [...numbers, ...moves];

  // If the key is not allowed, do not take it into account.
  // The event object is available here.
  if (!authorized.includes(event.key)) event.preventDefault();
}

</script>

<template>

<h3>MyCounter Component</h3>

Reactive variable count: <input type="text"
@keydown="verifyKey()" v-model="count" />
<br/><br/>
Entered value: <b>{{count}}</b>

</template>
```

The event-handling function verifyKey() uses the event object to determine the pressed key. The key property of the event object retrieves the code of the pressed key as a string:

- "Backspace": Represents the code for the backspace key

- "ArrowLeft" and "ArrowRight": Represent the codes for the left and right arrow keys

- "Delete": Represents the code for the Delete key

- "Tab": Represents the code for the Tab key (moves to the next field if it exists)

- "Home" and "End": Represent the codes for keys that go to the beginning or end of the input field

The numbers 0 to 9 are represented by the codes "0" to "9".

The main processing involves rejecting all keys that are not the allowed ones mentioned previously. For disallowed keys, the `event.preventDefault()` method of JavaScript is called, preventing the default event processing and therefore not taking the event into account. For all other allowed keys, the default processing is carried out (so the corresponding key is processed).

You can verify that only the keys from 0 to 9 are taken into account, as well as the arrow keys and field modification keys.

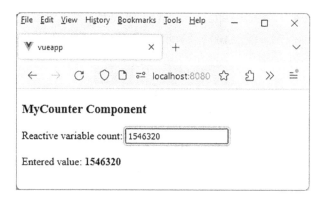

Figure 3-3. *Taking only digits into account in the field*

Step 2: Handling the Content of a Field

Let's enhance this program by displaying an error message if the value entered in the field is greater than 100.

155

We use the input event for this purpose, which is triggered when the key has been processed. If the value entered in the field is greater than 100, we display an error message using a reactive variable message initialized to "".

Do not exceed the value 100 in the input field (file src/components/ MyCounter.vue)

```
<script setup>

import { ref } from "vue"

const count = ref();
const message = ref("");

const verifyKey = () => {
  const numbers = ["0", "1", "2", "3", "4", "5", "6", "7",
  "8", "9"];
  const moves = ["Backspace", "ArrowLeft", "ArrowRight",
                 "Delete", "Tab", "Home", "End"];

  let authorized;  // Allowed keys in the input field
  authorized = [...numbers, ...moves];

  // If the key is not allowed, do not take it into account.
  // The event object is available here.
  if (!authorized.includes(event.key)) event.preventDefault();
}

const verifyMax100 = () => {
  message.value = "";
  // The event object is available here.
  if (parseInt(event.target.value) > 100) message.value = "Do
  not exceed 100!";
}
```

```
</script>

<template>

<h3>MyCounter Component</h3>

Reactive variable count: <input type="text" v-model="count"
    @keydown="verifyKey()"
    @input="verifyMax100()" />
<br/><br/>
Entered value: <b>{{count}}</b>
<br/><br/>
Message : <b>{{message}}</b>

</template>
```

During the input event, the value entered in the input field is available in the variable event.target.value. If this value is greater than 100, the reactive variable message is initialized with the text of the error message to be displayed; otherwise, the message is cleared.

For example, if you enter the value 101 in the input field, you can see the error message as shown in Figure 3-4.

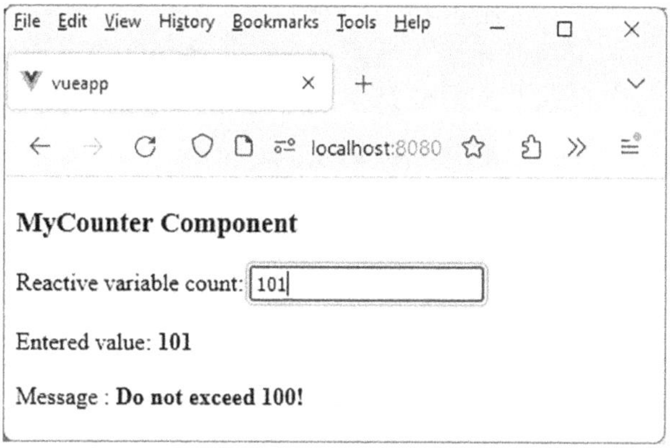

Figure 3-4. *Error message displayed if exceeding 100*

Step 3: Clearing the Field Content on Click

During a click in the input field, the current value is currently retained. Now, we want the field to be cleared upon clicking it so that a new value can be entered directly.

To achieve this, we need to handle the focus event on the input field.

Clear the field content on focus (file src/components/MyCounter.vue)

```
<script setup>

import { ref } from "vue"

const count = ref();
const message = ref("");

const verifyKey = () => {
  const numbers = ["0", "1", "2", "3", "4", "5", "6", "7",
  "8", "9"];
  const moves = ["Backspace", "ArrowLeft", "ArrowRight",
              "Delete", "Tab", "Home", "End"];

  let authorized;  // Allowed keys in the input field
  authorized = [...numbers, ...moves];

  // If the key is not allowed, do not take it into account.
  // The event object is available here.
  if (!authorized.includes(event.key)) event.preventDefault();
}
const verifyMax100 = () => {
  message.value = "";
  // The event object is available here.
```

```
  if (parseInt(event.target.value) > 100) message.value = "Do
  not exceed 100!";
}

const eraseField = () => {
  event.target.value = "";
  count.value = "";
  message.value = "";
}

</script>

<template>

<h3>MyCounter Component</h3>

Reactive variable count: <input type="text" v-model="count"
    @keydown="verifyKey()"
    @input="verifyMax100()"
    @focus="eraseField()" />
<br/><br/>
Entered value: <b>{{count}}</b>
<br/><br/>
Message : <b>{{message}}</b>

</template>
```

The field is now cleared upon clicking it:

Figure 3-5. *The content of the field is cleared on click*

Communication Between a Child Component and a Parent Component

When creating an application, it is common to need to transmit information to a child component or send information back to its parent component.

Vue.js enables this through the following:

- Props (or attributes) for transmitting information from the parent component to the child component

- Events for sending information from the child component to the parent component

Let's explore these two types of communication through an example.

Step 1: Communicating with a Child Component

Communication from a parent component to a child component is done using attributes that are passed to it.

We have already used this type of communication, for example, with the MyCounters component in the form <MyCounters :nb="3" />.

App Component (file src/App.vue)

```
<script setup>

import MyCounters from "./components/MyCounters.vue"

</script>

<template>

<MyCounters :nb="3" />

</template>
```

The App component (parent of the MyCounters component) here transmits the desired number of counters when displaying it.

Notice the use of :nb instead of just nb. Without the colon, the string "3" would be transmitted to the MyCounters component, rather than the JavaScript value 3 written within quotes.

The MyCounters component receives this new attribute and processes it using a v-for directive.

MyCounters Component (file src/components/MyCounters.vue)

```
<script setup>
import MyCounter from "./MyCounter.vue";
import { defineProps } from "vue";

const props = defineProps(["nb"]);
```

161

```
const nb = props.nb || 1;    // If the nb attribute is not
                             // specified, it defaults to 1.
```

```
</script>
```

```
<template>
```

```
<MyCounter v-for="i in nb" :key="i" :index="i"/>
```

```
</template>
```

If you transmit nb="3" instead of :nb="3" in the App component, you need to write the v-for directive as v-for="i in parseInt(nb)" to retrieve the value of the nb attribute as an integer.

The MyCounter component increments a reactive variable count upon clicking the "count+1" button.

MyCounter Component (file src/components/MyCounter.vue)

```
<script setup>
```

```
import { ref, defineProps } from "vue"
```

```
const count = ref(0);
const props = defineProps(["index"]);
const index = props.index || 1;
```

```
const increment = () => {
  count.value++;
}
```

```
</script>
```

```
<template>
```

```
<h3>{{index}} - MyCounter Component</h3>
```

```
Reactive variable count : <b>{{count}}</b>
```

```
<br/><br/>
<button @click="increment()">count+1</button>
<br/>

</template>
```

In Figure 3-6, you can see the display of the three counters.

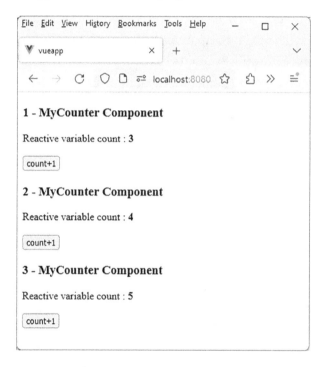

Figure 3-6. *Display of the three counters*

Each counter is independent of the others. Therefore, it is currently challenging to calculate the sum of the counters. Let's see how to proceed using events to communicate with the parent component.

Step 2: Communicating with the Parent Component

The sum of the counters is a variable that will be stored in the MyCounters component, which gathers all the counters. Each MyCounter component must notify the parent component, MyCounters, whenever an incrementation occurs on a counter. The MyCounter child component uses an event for this purpose, which the parent component, MyCounters, receives and processes.

First, let's see how the MyCounters parent component can receive and handle an event indicating that its overall total should be incremented.

MyCounters Component (file src/components/MyCounters.vue)

```
<script setup>
import MyCounter from "./MyCounter.vue";
import { ref, defineProps } from "vue";

const props = defineProps(["nb"]);
const nb = props.nb || 1;

const total = ref(0);

const increment = (value) => {
  total.value += value;
}

</script>

<template>

<MyCounter v-for="i in nb" :key="i" :index="i" @
incr="increment"/>
<br/><hr/><br/>
Overall Total : <b>{{total}}</b>

</template>
```

We added a reactive variable called `total` in the `MyCounters` component, which will be incremented upon receiving the `incr` event. Note the syntax `@incr="increment"` instead of `@incr="increment()"`. Using `"increment()"` would assume that the `increment()` function doesn't take any parameters. However, in this case, we want to pass the value parameter, which represents the increment value. Now, let's see how the child component `MyCounter` can transmit a value when triggering an event (in this case, the `incr` event) to the parent component.

MyCounter Component (file src/components/MyCounter.vue)

```
<script setup>

import { ref, defineProps, defineEmits } from "vue"

const count = ref(0);
const props = defineProps(["index"]);
const index = props.index || 1;

// We define the "incr" event to be used towards the parent
const emit = defineEmits(["incr"]);

const increment = () => {
  count.value++;
  emit("incr", 1);   // Sending the "incr" event with the value 1
}

</script>

<template>

<h3>{{index}} - MyCounter Component</h3>

Reactive variable count : <b>{{count}}</b>
<br/><br/>
```

```
<button @click="increment()">count+1</button>
<br/>

</template>
```

The defineEmits() method allows us to define one or more events that can be used in the component. The events are described as strings in an array, in this case, ["incr"].

Since the child component is transmitting a value during the incr event, it is necessary to receive the incr event in the parent using the syntax @incr="increment" and not @incr="increment()", which would not allow us to retrieve the transmitted value.

Let's verify that the total is updated correctly by clicking on each button:

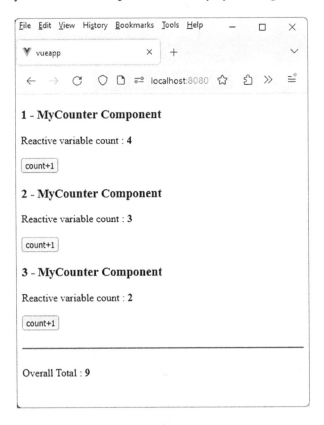

Figure 3-7. *Displaying the total of counters*

Using provide( ) and inject( ) for Communication Between Components

The mechanism we studied earlier, using events to communicate with the parent or props to communicate with children, is the basic mechanism offered by Vue.js. However, sometimes a different approach is desired, especially when a component needs to communicate not with its direct parent but with a parent further up in the hierarchy. This is also the case when you want to transmit props to components that are more distant than direct children.

Of course, this could be achieved by propagating events or passing attributes from child to child. However, intermediate components would then be involved in actions that don't concern them.

Vue.js provides an alternative system using the provide( ) and inject( ) methods:

- provide(name, value) is used to describe what a component makes available, under the name name, for its child components (direct or further down the hierarchy). This can include reactive variables, attributes (props), methods, etc.

- inject(name) allows a component in the descendant tree to specify what it wants to use, provided by a parent component through provide(name).

Elements made available by provide( ) can be accessed by child components that request them using inject( ).

To illustrate this, let's revisit the previous example. We modify the App component by integrating the reactive variable total and removing it from the MyCounters component. Now, each click on the "count+1" button in the MyCounter component needs to update the total variable located not in the MyCounters parent component but in the root App component.

Step 1: Using the provide( ) Method

We use the provide(name, value) method to make the total variable available for the descendants. This value becomes accessible to all components in the descendant tree.

The App component can be written as follows:

App Component (src/App.vue file)

```
<script setup>
import MyCounters from "./components/MyCounters.vue"

import { ref, provide } from "vue";

const total = ref(0);

// The total variable is made available for the descendants
under the name "total"
provide("total", total);

</script>

<template>

<MyCounters :nb="3" />
<br/><hr/><br/>
Overall Total: <b>{{total}}</b>

</template>
```

The "total" functionality made available can now be used in the descendants' components of the App component, including the MyCounter component. The inject() method is used to retrieve these functionalities in the component that will use them.

Step 2: Use the inject( ) Method

Now let's see how the functionalities provided by provide() are used. The inject() method allows us to retrieve them in the component that will use them. In this case, we use them in the MyCounter component. The MyCounters component is not affected and remains as simple as possible, just displaying the requested MyCounter components.

MyCounters Component (file src/components/MyCounters.vue)

```
<script setup>

import MyCounter from "./MyCounter.vue";
import { defineProps } from "vue";

const props = defineProps(["nb"]);
const nb = props.nb || 1;

</script>

<template>

<MyCounter v-for="i in nb" :key="i" :index="i" />

</template>
```

The MyCounter component is modified to use the "total" functionality provided by the App component. The "total" functionality is a reactive variable made available in the App component to be updated in the MyCounter component.

MyCounter Component (file src/components/MyCounter.vue)

```
<script setup>

import { ref, defineProps, inject } from "vue"

const count = ref(0);
```

```
const props = defineProps(["index"]);
const index = props.index || 1;
```

// Access to the "total" functionality (which is a reactive
variable)
const total = inject("total");

```
const increment = () => {
  count.value++;
  total.value++;
}
```

`</script>`

`<template>`

`<h3>{{index}} - MyCounter Component</h3>`

```
Reactive variable count: <b>{{count}}</b>
<br/><br/>
<button @click="increment()">count+1</button>
<br/>
```

`</template>`

Let's verify that it works:

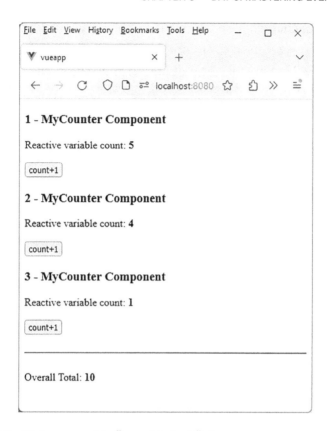

Figure 3-8. *Using provide() and inject() for component communication*

Conclusion

At this point, you've gained a solid understanding of the basics of Vue. js, including state and event management, directives, and components. However, modern web applications often don't operate in isolation; they frequently interact with remote servers to retrieve or send data.

In the next chapter, we'll take a crucial step forward by exploring how to make HTTP requests to communicate with a remote server. We'll put this knowledge into practice by building an application that retrieves and displays a list of all countries worldwide using a REST API. You'll also learn how to filter this data based on user input.

CHAPTER 4

Day 4: Building an Application in Vue.js

In this chapter, we'll delve into a fundamental aspect of modern web development: communication between the client and server via HTTP requests. You'll learn how to make requests to retrieve data from a remote server and use it in your Vue.js application.

We'll build a practical application to implement these concepts. The application will display a list of all countries worldwide, allowing the user to filter this list based on the characters entered in a search field. To achieve this, we'll use the REST API available at the following URL: `https://restcountries.com/v3.1/all`.

So not only will you reinforce your Vue.js skills, but you'll also acquire new skills in JSON data manipulation and interacting with REST APIs.

Introduction to the REST API

The list of countries is retrieved from the following URL: `https://restcountries.com/v3.1/all`. If you enter this URL into a browser, you'll receive a JSON-formatted response like the following:

© Eric Sarrion 2024
E. Sarrion, *Master Vue.js in 6 Days*, https://doi.org/10.1007/979-8-8688-0364-2_4

Figure 4-1. *Response from the URL* `https://restcountries.com/`
`v3.1/all`

The displayed response shows that the provided data corresponds to an array of JavaScript objects, containing detailed information about each country.

The goal of this example will be to make an HTTP request to this server and then display the response in a browser as a list.

Application Screens

Here, we describe all the screens of the application, based on user actions.

Upon launching the application, the list of countries is retrieved (Figure 4-2) and displayed (Figure 4-3):

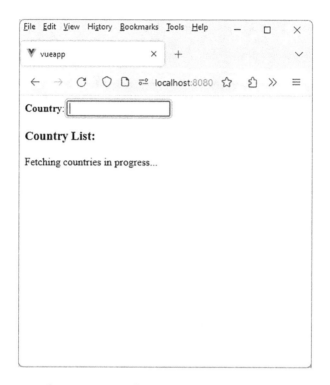

Figure 4-2. *Fetching country list*

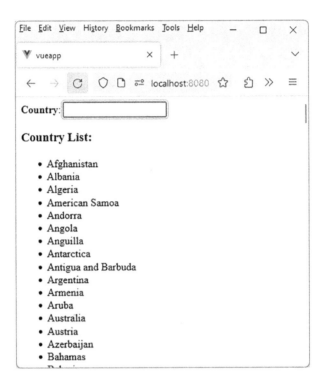

Figure 4-3. *Country list retrieved and displayed*

The "Country" input field allows entering the beginning of a country name. The displayed countries in Figure 4-4 will then be those whose names start with the entered letters.

If you type "e" in the field, only countries whose names start with "e" will be displayed:

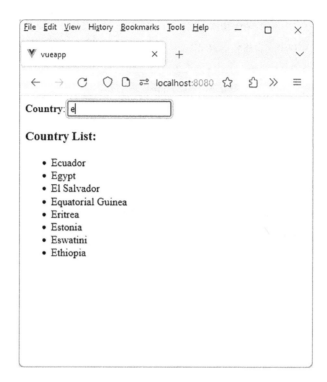

Figure 4-4. *The list of countries is filtered based on the entered beginning of the country's name*

The list updates as the input is entered.

Let's see how to implement this application with Vue.js. We'll start by breaking down the application into components.

Breaking Down the Application into Components

The application will consist of two components:

1. The App component containing the overall application. It will include an input field for the country name and a MyCountries component containing the list of countries.

2. The MyCountries component that contains the list of countries and displays those whose names start with the letters entered in the country name field (from the App component).

To achieve this, the MyCountries component should have an attribute representing the entered country name in the App component. The MyCountries component will automatically refresh whenever the country name is modified in the input field.

We can start writing the App and MyCountries components as follows:

App component (src/App.vue file)

```
<script setup>

import MyCountries from './components/MyCountries.vue'

import { ref } from "vue";

const name = ref("");

</script>

<template>

<b>Country</b>: <input type="text" v-model="name" />
<br>
<MyCountries :name="name" />

</template>
```

The country name input field is associated with a reactive variable, name, updated as the input progresses through the v-model directive. This reactive variable name is passed as an attribute to the MyCountries component, which will be automatically updated whenever the attribute's value changes.

The MyCountries component is outlined here in a concise manner. Currently, it simply displays the value of the name attribute passed to it, along with the "Retrieving countries..." message displayed until the list of countries is retrieved.

MyCountries component (src/components/MyCountries.vue file)

```
<script setup>

import { defineProps, ref } from "vue";
defineProps(["name"]);

const names = ref([]);    // Countries names displayed in
                          // the list
let countries= [];        // All country names (retrieved only
                          // once at startup)

</script>

<template>

<h3>Country List</h3>

<div v-show="!countries.length">Fetching countries in
progress...</div>
Entered Country: {{name}}
<ul>
<li v-for="n in names" :key="n" >{{n}}</li>
</ul>

</template>
```

Let's make some observations about the code of the `MyCountries` component:

1. The `name` attribute is retrieved using `defineProps(["name"])` and then displayed in the `<template>` with `{{name}}`. Indeed, this ensures that communication between the App component and the `MyCountries` component is established.

2. The "Fetching countries in progress ..." waiting text will be displayed only when the list of countries has not been retrieved yet. This is achieved using the `v-show` directive with the condition `"!countries.length"`, meaning that the associated `<div>` is displayed only if the retrieved list of countries is empty.

3. The reactive variable `names` contains the list of all retrieved countries and is updated based on the value of the transmitted `name` attribute. It is displayed as a list `<li>` with a `v-for` directive.

4. The `countries` variable represents the list of all country names, retrieved only once during the application's launch.

Let's examine the result produced by the implementation of these two components:

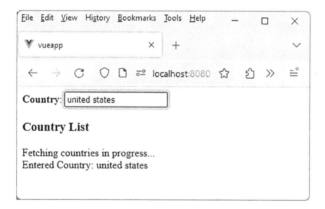

Figure 4-5. *Application launch (temporary)*

If we type the beginning of a name in the input field, it should be displayed in the `MyCountries` component. This demonstrates that attribute-based communication between the `App` component and the `MyCountries` component is functioning:

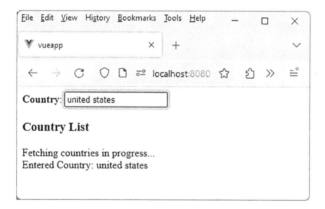

Figure 4-6. *Entering the name of a country*

The foundational components are created. Now, let's enhance them to finalize our application.

Retrieving the List of Countries

Let's start by fetching and displaying the list of countries. This list is retrieved only once, at the application's startup. We perform this operation in the MyCountries component. To ensure it happens only once at startup, we decide to do it in the onMounted() method, which is called when the component is mounted in the DOM.

Retrieve the list of country names (src/components/MyCountries. vue file)

```
<script setup>

import { defineProps, ref, onMounted } from "vue";
defineProps(["name"]);

const names = ref([]);    // Countries names displayed in
                          the list
let countries= [];        // All country names (retrieved only
                          once at startup)

onMounted(() => {
  var url = "https://restcountries.com/v3.1/all";
  fetch(url)
  .then((res) => res.text())
  .then((data) => {
    countries = JSON.parse(data).map(function(elem) {
      return elem.name.common;
    });
    // In ascending alphabetical order
    countries = countries.sort((n1, n2) => {
      if (n1 > n2) return 1;
      if (n1 < n2) return -1;
      return 0;
```

```
  });
  names.value = countries;      // Updating the displayed list.
})
.catch((err) => names.value = [err.toString()]);
});
```

</script>

<template>

<h3>Country List:</h3>

<div v-show="!countries.length">Fetching countries in
progress...</div>
<ul>
<li v-for="n in names" :key="n" >{{n}}</li>
</ul>

</template>

We utilize the JavaScript fetch(url) method to make a request to a server. The server's response is then transformed and placed into an alphabetically sorted array called countries.

Please note that we use elem.name.common to retrieve the country's name. You can see it by looking at Figure 4-1 that displays the full JSON response.

This array is subsequently transferred to the reactive variable names, which is displayed as a list using the v-for directive in the <template> section of the component. Additionally, since the countries array will be populated with at least one element, the "Fetching countries in progress..." waiting text will be hidden, and the list of countries will be displayed.

In this context, we have employed JavaScript promises, utilizing the then() and catch() methods. An alternative version of this program utilizes JavaScript's async and await instructions.

Using async and await instructions (src/components/MyCountries. vue file)

```
<script setup>

import { defineProps, ref, onMounted } from "vue";
defineProps(["name"]);

const names = ref([]);   // Countries names displayed in
                         the list
let countries= [];       // All country names (retrieved only
                         once at startup)

async function getCountries() {
  var url = "https://restcountries.com/v3.1/all";
  var response = await fetch(url);
  var data = await response.text();
  countries = JSON.parse(data).map(function(elem) {
    return elem.name.common;
  });
  // In ascending alphabetical order
  countries = countries.sort((n1, n2) => {
    if (n1 > n2) return 1;
    if (n1 < n2) return -1;
    return 0;
  });
  return countries;
}
```

```
onMounted(async () => {
  names.value = await getCountries();
});
```

```
</script>
```

```
<template>
```

```
<h3>Country List:</h3>
```

```
<div v-show="!countries.length">Fetching countries in
progress...</div>
<ul>
<li v-for="n in names" :key="n" >{{n}}</li>
</ul>
```

```
</template>
```

We have created the function getCountries() as an asynchronous function, called directly in the onMounted() method using the async and await instructions. Regardless of the program version used, the list of countries is retrieved and then displayed:

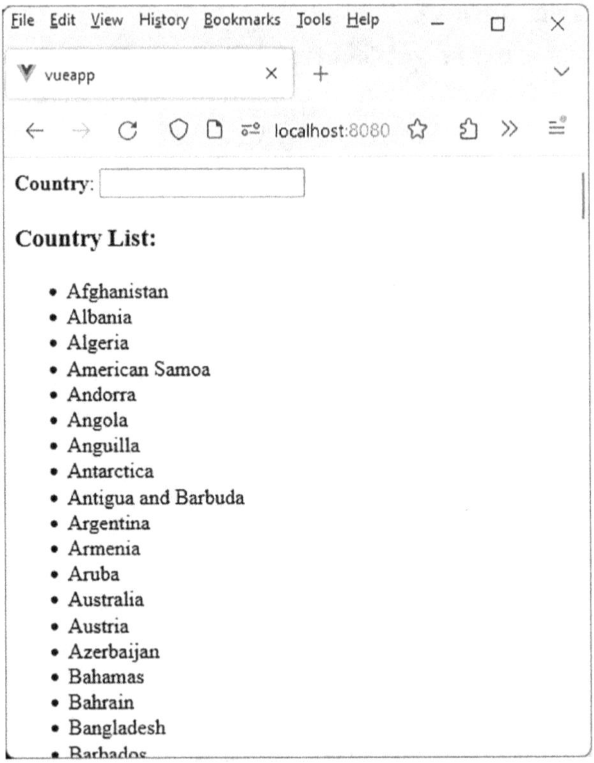

Figure 4-7. *Retrieved and displayed list of countries*

The list of countries is now successfully retrieved and displayed. Let's now explore how to filter the list based on the entered beginning of the country's name in the Country field.

Filtering the List of Countries According to the Entered Name

Currently, entering characters in the country name field does not produce any changes to the displayed list. This is expected because the MyCountries component does not yet consider the name attribute that is passed to it.

To filter the list of countries based on the entered name, you would need to execute the following code block:

Filter the list based on the entered name

```
let countriesFiltered = countries.filter((n) => {
  // Construct the regular expression (regex)
  const reg = new RegExp("^" + props.name, "i");
  if (n.match(reg)) return true;    // We keep the name in
                                    the list
  else return false;                // We do not keep the name
                                    in the list
});
names.value = countriesFiltered;    // Update the displayed list
```

Let's provide some explanations for this code block:

1. The variable `countriesFiltered` contains an array of country names constructed from the initial `countries` array. For example, if we want to keep in the list the names of countries starting with `"fr"`, we use the regular expression `"^fr"`, where `"fr"` is the word transmitted in the name attribute and therefore included in `props.name`.

2. The `"i"` parameter used as the second argument in the `RegExp` class signifies case insensitivity, meaning it ignores uppercase or lowercase distinctions in country names.

3. The `filter()` method returns a new array, indicating whether to keep (`return true`) or reject (`return false`) the initial element.

4.   It then remains to update the reactive variable `names`
with this new list of country names, which is done
by writing `names.value = countriesFiltered`.

Now, the question arises as to where to place this code block.
One might be tempted to place it in the `onUpdated()` method of the
component, which is called when the component is updated, but that's not
a good idea. Updating the reactive variable `names` in this part of the code
would result in an infinite loop because it would trigger a new update of
the component, leading to a new call to the `onUpdated()` method.

To avoid such issues, Vue.js has created the `watch()` method, which
allows you to perform a task when a variable is updated. The observed
variable here will be `props.name`, which is the value of the `name` attribute in
the `MyCountries` component.

Using the watch( ) Method

The `watch(name, callback)` method allows observing changes that occur
on a reactive variable named `name` and invoking the processing function
`callback(newValue, oldValue)` when a change occurs:

- The `newValue` parameter corresponds to the new value
  of the observed reactive variable.

- The `oldValue` parameter corresponds to the old value
  of the observed reactive variable.

The `watch()` method is typically employed to monitor changes on
a reactive variable, but it will be demonstrated that it is also possible
to observe nonreactive variables (such as `props.name`) using the
`watch()` method.

Let's write the previous code block in a `watch()` function for `props.`
`name` using the `watch()` method:

MyCountries component (src/components/MyCountries.vue file)

```
<script setup>

import { defineProps, ref, onMounted, watch } from "vue";
const props = defineProps(["name"]);

const names = ref([]);      // Countries names displayed in
                            // the list
let countries= [];          // All country names (retrieved only
                            // once at startup)

onMounted(() => {
  var url = "https://restcountries.com/v3.1/all";
  fetch(url)
  .then((res) => res.text())
  .then((data) => {
    countries = JSON.parse(data).map(function(elem) {
      return elem.name.common;
    });
    // In ascending alphabetical order
    countries = countries.sort((n1, n2) => {
      if (n1 > n2) return 1;
      if (n1 < n2) return -1;
      return 0;
    });
    names.value = countries;

  })
  .catch((err) => names.value = [err.toString()]);
});

watch(props.name, (newName) => {
  let countriesFiltered = countries.filter((n) => {
    const reg = new RegExp("^" + newName, "i");
```

```
    if (n.match(reg)) return true;
    else return false;
  });
  names.value = countriesFiltered;
});
```

</script>

<template>

<h3>Country List:</h3>

<div v-show="!countries.length">Fetching countries in
progress...</div>
<ul>
<li v-for="n in names" :key="n" >{{n}}</li>
</ul>

</template>

Indeed, it's crucial to test the functionality. Let's run the program and enter characters in the input field to verify its operation.

Figure 4-8. *The list of countries does not update*

It appears that the filter is not working. The explanation is as follows.

When we write watch(props.name, callback), we are observing the value of the variable props.name at the moment the watch() function is written, that is, during initialization (or setup). However, as the variable props.name is not reactive, it would be necessary to update the value of props.name based on what is entered in the input field.

To achieve this, we need to create a "getter" function that retrieves the current value of props.name. This can be simply written as ()=>props.name.

Therefore, we write the following:

MyCountries component (src/components/MyCountries.vue file)

```
<script setup>

import { defineProps, ref, onMounted, watch } from "vue";
const props = defineProps(["name"]);

const names = ref([]);    // Countries names displayed in
                          // the list
let countries= [];        // All country names (retrieved only
                          // once at startup)

onMounted(() => {
  var url = "https://restcountries.com/v3.1/all";
  fetch(url)
  .then((res) => res.text())
  .then((data) => {
    countries = JSON.parse(data).map(function(elem) {
      return elem.name.common;
    });
    // In ascending alphabetical order
    countries = countries.sort((n1, n2) => {
      if (n1 > n2) return 1;
      if (n1 < n2) return -1;
      return 0;
    });
    names.value = countries;

  })
  .catch((err) => names.value = [err.toString()]);
});

watch(()=>props.name, (newName) => {
```

```
  let countriesFiltered = countries.filter((n) => {
    const reg = new RegExp("^" + newName, "i");
    if (n.match(reg)) return true;
    else return false;
  });
  names.value = countriesFiltered;
});
```

```
</script>
```

```
<template>
```

```
<h3>Country List:</h3>
```

```
<div v-show="!countries.length">Fetching countries in
progress...</div>
<ul>
<li v-for="n in names" :key="n" >{{n}}</li>
</ul>
```

```
</template>
```

Indeed, using the notation ()=>props.name returns the current value of props.name, allowing it to be observed and compared to the previous value. Let's verify that this works:

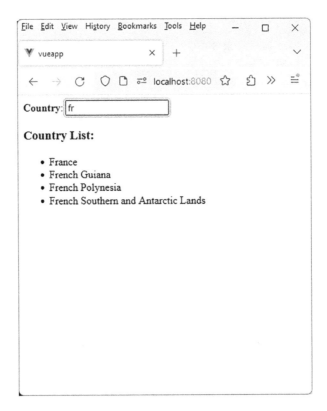

Figure 4-9. *Functional country filter*

We have successfully filtered the list based on the characters entered by the user in the input field. The watch() method helped us achieve this. Vue.js also offers another filtering method, which is the watchEffect() method. Let's see how to use it for list filtering.

Using the watchEffect( ) Method

The watchEffect(callback) method is similar to the previously discussed watch(name, callback) method, with some differences.

Instead of specifying the name of the observed variable in the parameters, the observed variables (*reactive or not*) will be those used in the callback function. Vue.js executes the callback function at each component initialization to determine the variables that will be observed.

If variables are used in a part of the callback function that is not executed at startup, these variables will not be observed and will not trigger future executions of the callback function.

The `watchEffect()` method can be summarized in three points:

1. **Automatic Dependency Detection**: Unlike `watch()`, which requires explicitly specifying the variables to observe, `watchEffect(callback)` automatically detects variables accessed in the callback function.

2. **Initial Execution**: `watchEffect(callback)` executes the callback function once during component initialization to identify the variables to observe.

3. **Unexecuted Parts**: If variables are present in code parts that are not executed during initialization (e.g., in an unexecuted conditional branch), these variables will not be recorded as dependencies and will not trigger future executions of the callback function.

Let's use the `watchEffect()` method instead of the previous `watch()` method. We want to observe the `props.name` variable in `watchEffect()` to modify the list based on the entered country name. For this, this variable must be used during the first execution of the callback function, which occurs at the initialization of the `MyCountries` component.

If we replace the direct call to the `watch()` method with that of the `watchEffect()` method, it is written as follows:

**Using the watchEffect() method (file src/components/
MyCountries.vue)**

```
<script setup>

import { defineProps, ref, onMounted, watchEffect } from "vue";
const props = defineProps(["name"]);

const names = ref([]);    // Countries names displayed in
                          the list
let countries= [];        // All country names (retrieved only
                          once at startup)

onMounted(() => {
  var url = "https://restcountries.com/v3.1/all";
  fetch(url)
  .then((res) => res.text())
  .then((data) => {
    countries = JSON.parse(data).map(function(elem) {
      return elem.name.common;
    });
    // In ascending alphabetical order
    countries = countries.sort((n1, n2) => {
      if (n1 > n2) return 1;
      if (n1 < n2) return -1;
      return 0;
    });
    names.value = countries;

  })
  .catch((err) => names.value = [err.toString()]);
});

watchEffect(() => {
  let countriesFiltered = countries.filter((n) => {
```

```
  const reg = new RegExp("^" + props.name, "i");
  if (n.match(reg)) return true;
  else return false;
});
names.value = countriesFiltered;
});

</script>

<template>

<h3>Country List:</h3>

<div v-show="!countries.length">Fetching countries in
progress...</div>
<ul>
<li v-for="n in names" :key="n" >{{n}}</li>
</ul>

</template>
```

One can verify that this does not work, and it is expected, as for
the variable props.name to be within a code block executed during
the component initialization, the filter() method would need to be
executed, which is not the case here because the countries array is
initially empty.

A workaround involves the inclusion of the statement console.
log(props.name), effectively allowing the utilization of the variable props.
name for subsequent observation. The modification to the watchEffect()
method is as follows:

Use console.log(props.name) within watchEffect()

```
watchEffect(() => {
  console.log(props.name); // Do not delete: allows the
                           observation of props.name
```

```
let countriesFiltered = countries.filter((n) => {
  const reg = new RegExp("^" + props.name, "i");
  if (n.match(reg)) return true;
  else return false;
});
names.value = countriesFiltered;
});
```

Let's verify that the variable props.name is now being observed:

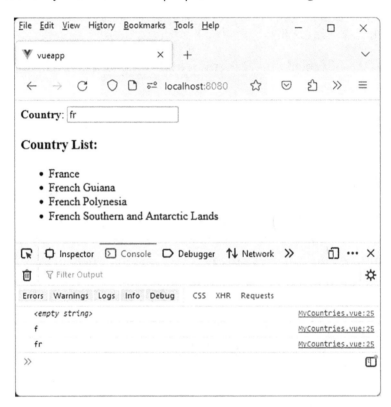

Figure 4-10. *The variable props.name is observed by watchEffect()*

To provide comprehensive explanations, another way to filter the list can also be offered, using the provide() and inject() methods, which enable data sharing between multiple components. Let's explore how to use them here.

Using the provide( ) and inject( ) Methods

An alternative program structure is possible by employing the provide() and inject() methods.

Instead of passing the reactive variable name as an attribute to MyCountries, it is transmitted from the App component through the provide() method and retrieved in the MyCountries component using the inject() method.

The App component becomes the following:

App component (file src/App.vue)

```
<script setup>

import MyCountries from './components/MyCountries.vue'

import { ref, provide } from "vue";

const name = ref("");
provide("name", name);

</script>

<template>

<b>Country</b>: <input type="text" v-model="name" />
<br>
<MyCountries />

</template>
```

The MyCountries component is now used without the name attribute. However, this reactive variable is transmitted to child components using the provide("name", name) method and will be retrieved in the MyCountries component through the inject("name") method.

The MyCountries component is modified as follows:

MyCountries component (file src/components/MyCountries.vue)

```
<script setup>

import { ref, onMounted, watch, inject } from "vue";

const names = ref([]);    // Countries names displayed in
                          the list
let countries= [];        // All country names (retrieved only
                          once at startup)

const name = inject("name");    // The reactive variable name is
retrieved


onMounted(() => {
  var url = "https://restcountries.com/v3.1/all";
  fetch(url)
  .then((res) => res.text())
  .then((data) => {
    countries = JSON.parse(data).map(function(elem) {
      return elem.name.common;
    });
    // In ascending alphabetical order
    countries = countries.sort((n1, n2) => {
      if (n1 > n2) return 1;
      if (n1 < n2) return -1;
      return 0;
    });
```

```
    names.value = countries;
  })
  .catch((err) => names.value = [err.toString()]);
});

watch(name, () => {
  let countriesFiltered = countries.filter((n) => {
    const reg = new RegExp("^" + name.value, "i");
    if (n.match(reg)) return true;
    else return false;
  });
  names.value = countriesFiltered;
});
```

```
</script>
```

```
<template>
```

```
<h3>Country List:</h3>
```

```
<div v-show="!countries.length">Fetching countries in
progress...</div>
<ul>
<li v-for="n in names" :key="n" >{{n}}</li>
</ul>
```

```
</template>
```

The reactive variable name can be directly observed using the watch(name, callback) method, as it is indeed the reactive variable name being observed here, and not an attribute transmitted via props.name as before. Let's verify that this works:

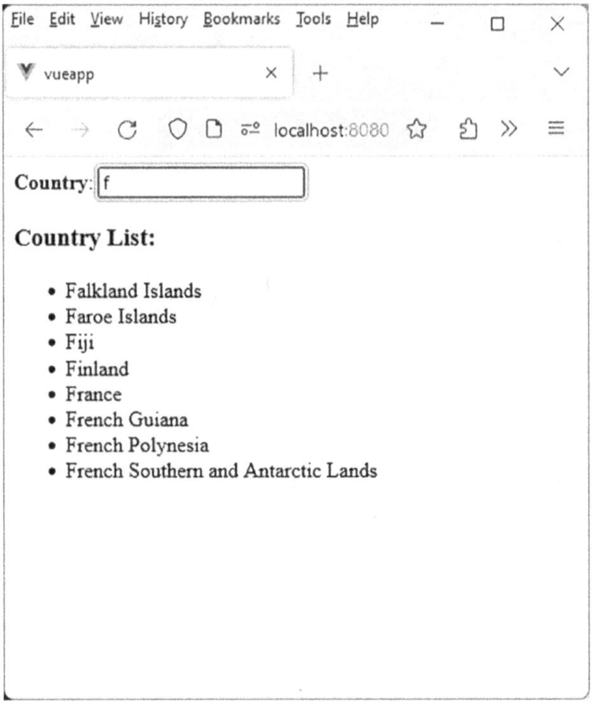

Figure 4-11. *Usage of provide() and inject()*

Giving Focus to the Input Field

The program can be further enhanced by giving focus to the input field as soon as the page is displayed. The focus() method provided by the DOM API is employed for this purpose.

It is necessary to modify the App component that contains the input field to which focus should be given. The onMounted() method is utilized to access the DOM element corresponding to the input field.

Giving focus to the input field (file src/App.vue)

```
<script setup>

import MyCountries from './components/MyCountries.vue'

import { ref, provide, onMounted } from "vue";

const name = ref("");
provide("name", name);

onMounted(()=>document.querySelector("input[type=text]").
focus());

</script>

<template>

<b>Country</b>: <input type="text" v-model="name" />
<br>
<MyCountries />

</template>
```

The input field is accessed through the DOM API, for example, by using document.querySelector(selector). All that remains is to use the focus() method of the DOM API on this element to give it focus.

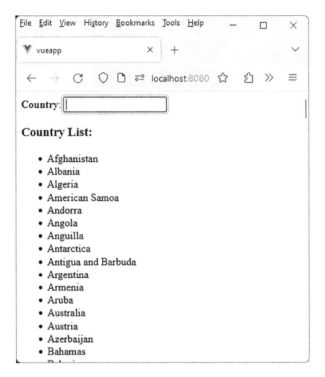

Figure 4-12. *The input field gains focus directly*

In the next chapter, we will explore the creation of a new directive that directly gives focus to the input field, providing a more optimal approach.

Conclusion

You now have a comprehensive understanding of how to perform HTTP requests in a Vue.js application. You have learned to retrieve data from a remote server and seamlessly integrate it into your application. The example of the country list has allowed you to implement these concepts, providing you with a practical and concrete experience.

While we have explored leveraging data from an external source, the upcoming chapter will take you further into customizing and optimizing Vue.js applications. We will delve into creating new directives and composables, powerful tools that enable you to build advanced features and efficiently reuse your application logic. These techniques will make your code both cleaner and more functional.

CHAPTER 5

Day 5: Mastering the Creation of Directives in Vue.js

We have covered the main features of Vue.js. Now, let's explore how these features can be extended by creating new directives. Vue.js provides standard directives such as `v-show`, `v-if`, `v-for`, `v-bind`, or `v-on`. It is possible to create custom directives tailored for use in our application components.

Why Create New Directives?

Creating custom directives offers several advantages that can significantly enhance code quality and maintainability. Some of these benefits include the following:

1. **Code Reusability**: Encapsulate frequently used behaviors into a directive and reuse them across multiple components.

2. **Clarity and Readability**: Using a well-named directive makes the template more readable and expressive.

3. **Testability**: Directives can be independently tested, facilitating the verification of their correct functionality.

4. **Extensibility**: Easily extend existing directive functionalities or create new directives for custom behaviors.

The ability to create custom directives promotes good code organization, reusability, and readability.

Now that we understand the usefulness of writing custom directives, let's delve into how to organize the code that will be executed when the directive is used.

Directive Lifecycle

A Vue.js directive is a JavaScript object that can have one or more of the following lifecycle properties. Each property is a method called at different stages of the lifecycle of the DOM element to which the directive is applied. This allows for the execution of specific actions at each stage:

1. `beforeMount(el, binding)`: Called just before the element `el` is inserted into the DOM

2. `mounted(el, binding)`: Called when the element `el` has just been added to the DOM

3. `beforeUpdate(el, binding)`: Called before the element `el` is updated, for example, when a reactive variable changes

4. `updated(el, binding)`: Called after the element `el` has been updated

5. `beforeUnmount(el, binding)`: Called just before the element `el` is removed from the DOM

6. `unmounted(el, binding)`: Called after the element `el` has been removed from the DOM

The primary method used among the aforementioned is the `mounted()` method. It runs once when the `el` element is attached to the DOM.

By using these methods, you can perform specific actions at different moments in the lifecycle of the element to which the directive is applied.

Each of these methods accepts two parameters: `el` and `binding`:

`el`: The DOM element associated with the directive (the one on which the directive is placed).

`binding`: An object containing additional information about the directive. This object can have several properties, such as the following:

- `binding.value`: The value passed to the directive (the value is indicated after the "=" sign if present after the directive).

- `binding.arg`: The argument passed to the directive, if used. The argument is separated by the ":" character with the directive. Only one argument can be specified. For example, for the `v-bind:value` directive, `binding.arg` is `"value"`.

- `binding.modifiers`: An object representing the modifiers applied to the directive. Multiple modifiers can be specified, separated by ".".

- `binding.instance`: The instance of the component using the directive.

- `binding.dir`: An object containing information about the directive itself.

209

One might ask: Where to place a directive?

According to the official Vue.js documentation, directives are primarily designed to be applied to DOM nodes, that is, HTML elements. Although it is possible to apply a directive to a Vue.js component, this use is not explicitly encouraged or recommended by Vue.js.

Creating a New Directive

To create a new directive, we use the `app.directive(name, callback)` method. The `app` object is returned by the `createApp(App)` method. The `createApp(App)` method is used in the `src/main.js` file of the application and is used to create the Vue.js application.

The newly created directives will be centralized from the `src/main.js` file. They can be either directly specified in this file or imported from a file that contains them. Let's explore these two possibilities by creating a `focus` directive that will be used in the form of `v-focus` in the component templates. This `v-focus` directive is designed to give focus to the HTML element to which it is applied, such as an input field.

Note that we define the directive in JavaScript programs under the name `focus` but use it in templates with the name `v-focus`.

Step 1: Creating the Directive in the src/main.js File

Let's start with the simplest case of inserting the `focus` directive directly into the `src/main.js` file. The `src/main.js` file becomes as follows:

Focus directive (file src/main.js)

```
import { createApp } from 'vue';
import App from './App.vue';
```

```
const focusDirective = {
  mounted(el) {
    el.focus();
  }
};
```

```
const app = createApp(App);
```

```
// Creation of the directive within the application
app.directive("focus", focusDirective);
```

```
app.mount('#app');
```

The file main.js is modified to retrieve the value of the variable app returned by the createApp(App) method. Subsequently, the app. directive() method is employed to create a new directive usable within the application.

The mounted(el) method is utilized to define the directive. This method is invoked in the lifecycle of the directive when the associated DOM element el is inserted into the DOM.

The directive is then employed in the MyCounter component, which displays an input field with the v-focus directive applied.

MyCounter component (file src/components/MyCounter.vue)

```
<script setup>
</script>
```

```
<template>
```

```
<h3>MyCounter Component</h3>
Counter value : <input v-focus />
```

```
</template>
```

The App component displays the MyCounter component:

App component (file src/App.vue)

```
<script setup>

import MyCounter from './components/MyCounter.vue'

</script>

<template>
```

<MyCounter />

```
</template>
```

Let's launch the application. The input field gains focus automatically without the need for a click.

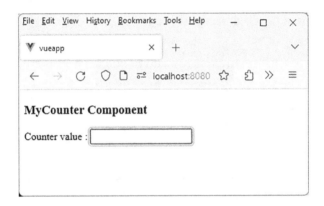

Figure 5-1. *Directive v-focus*

We have seen how to insert the new directive directly into the src/
main.js file. However, it is more practical to use another file to avoid
modifying, for each added directive, this crucial file for the application's
operation.

Step 2: Creating the Directive in a Directives File

Let's now explore another way of defining directives without having to modify the src/main.js file for each new directive added, as done previously.

Create the src/directives.js file that will contain our new directives. This file will be imported into the src/main.js file. Modify the src/main.js file to consider the directives defined in the src/directives.js file.

The src/directives.js file containing the focus directive is as follows:

Focus directive (file src/directives.js)

```
const focusDirective = {
  mounted(el) {
    el.focus();
  }
};

export default {
  focus : focusDirective,
}
```

The directive is defined as an object, focusDirective, as previously explained. The export default statement is used to convey this functionality to files that utilize it. In this case, it is the src/main.js file that leverages the content of src/directives.js. Here is the description of this file:

Creating the directives defined in src/directives.js (file src/main.js)

```
import { createApp } from 'vue';
import App from './App.vue';
import directives from "./directives.js"
```

```
const app = createApp(App);

for (let name in directives) {
  // Creation of the directive name within the application
  app.directive(name, directives[name]);
}

app.mount('#app');
```

The directives.js file is imported, and the obtained directives variable is an object of the form { focus, ... }. We iterate through the properties of this object and use the app.directive(name) method on each property name of the object. This way, only the src/directives.js file will be modified later to add new directives. The src/main.js file will no longer need modification when adding a new directive.

However, it is even more advantageous to place each directive in a separate file, as explained in the following.

Step 3: Creating the Directive in a Separate File

A variation of the previously created directives file would be to externalize each directive into a separate file. The src/directives.js file would then only need to import the external file associated with each directive.

Let's create the focus.js file associated with the v-focus directive. Also, create the src/directives directory that will contain files for each directive, each created in a separate file.

Focus directive (file src/directives/focus.js)

```
const focusDirective = {
  mounted(el) {
    el.focus();
  }
```

214

```
};
```

```
export default focusDirective;
```

The directive file must be imported into the `src/directives.js` file:

Importing the focus directive (file src/directives.js)

```
import focus from "./directives/focus";

export default {
  focus,
}
```

If you want to import other directives, you just need to add them to the `src/directives.js` file in the same manner. The other files, `App.vue` and `MyCounter.vue`, remain identical to the previous versions. The functionality remains unchanged.

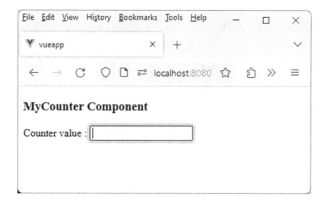

Figure 5-2. *Directive v-focus in a separate file*

To ensure greater maintainability of our Vue.js applications, this latter solution of writing directives in separate files offers better prospects for evolution. Let's now explore some examples of writing directives using the various possibilities offered by Vue.js.

Directive v-integers-only Allowing Only Numerical Input

Let's illustrate our examples by creating a new directive that allows only numerical input in an input field. We will name this directive `v-integers-only`.

We will use this directive in different forms:

1. `v-integers-only`: This is the simplest form of the directive. Used in this way, the directive signifies that only digits from 0 to 9 can be used in the input field.

2. `v-integers-only.hexa`: When the `hexa` modifier is used, it means modifying the basic behavior of the directive to also allow hexadecimal characters, that is, the letters from "a" to "f" or "A" to "F".

3. `v-integers-only.hexa.upper`: The `upper` modifier is used here in addition to the `hexa` modifier. It means replacing, during input, the characters "a" to "f" with the characters "A" to "F". Thus, the input "123abc" becomes "123ABC".

Let's see how to write these different forms of using the `v-integers-only` directive.

Step 1: Directive in the Form v-integers-only

Let's start by writing the simplest form of the directive. When this directive is present for an input field, it only allows entering digits from 0 to 9 in the field. Any other character, except for movement arrows, is not considered.

Note that we had already created a component that only allowed entering digits in the input field (see Chapter 3). However, we used events to manage the input field, which complicated the writing of the component. Here, we propose moving the event handling to the directive rather than the component.

As a reminder, the MyCounter component was as follows:

MyCounter component (file src/components/MyCounter.vue)

```
<script setup>

import { ref } from "vue"

const count = ref();

const verifyKey = () => {
  const numbers = ["0", "1", "2", "3", "4", "5", "6", "7",
  "8", "9"];
  const moves = ["Backspace", "ArrowLeft", "ArrowRight",
                "Delete", "Tab", "Home", "End"];

  let authorized;  // Allowed keys in the input field
  authorized = [...numbers, ...moves];

  // If the key is not allowed, do not take it into account.
  // The event object is available here.
  if (!authorized.includes(event.key)) event.preventDefault();
}

</script>

<template>

<h3>MyCounter Component</h3>

Reactive variable count: <input type="text"
@keydown="verifyKey()" v-model="count" />
```

```
<br/><br/>
Entered value: <b>{{count}}</b>

</template>
```

The verifyKey() method, placed on the <input> element, filtered keyboard keys to allow only digits or movement and deletion keys.

Let's create a directive that performs the same treatment. For this purpose, we create the directive file src/directives/integers-only.js, which is then included in the global src/directives.js file.

Directive v-integers-only (file src/directives/integers-only.js)

```
const integersOnly = {
  mounted(el) {
    el.addEventListener("keydown", (event) => {
      const numbers = ["0", "1", "2", "3", "4", "5", "6", "7",
                       "8", "9"];
      const moves = ["Backspace", "ArrowLeft", "ArrowRight",
                     "Delete", "Tab", "Home", "End"];

      let authorized;  // Allowed keys in the input field
      authorized = [...numbers, ...moves];

      // If the key is not allowed, do not take it into account.
      // The event object is available here.
      if (!authorized.includes(event.key)) event.preventDefault();
    });
  },
}

export default integersOnly;
```

We use the addEventListener() method defined in the DOM to listen for the keydown event on the DOM element el passed as a parameter to the mounted(el) method. The rest of the directive's program is similar to what was done when writing the MyCounter component.

The directive is integrated into the directives file src/directives.js:

Adding the directive to the directives file (file src/directives.js)

```
import focus from "./directives/focus";
import integersOnly from "./directives/integers-only";

export default {
  focus,
  integersOnly,   // It will be used in the form of
                  v-integers-only
}
```

The directive is exported as integersOnly but will be used in the form v-integers-only. Note that using it as v-integersOnly also works but is not recommended.

We use this directive in the MyCounter component, which becomes simpler than before:

Using the v-integers-only directive (file src/components/ MyCounter.vue)

```
<script setup>

import { ref } from "vue"

const count = ref();

</script>

<template>

<h3>MyCounter Component</h3>
```

Reactive variable count: **<input type="text" v-focus v-integers-only v-model="count" />**

`<br/><br/>`

Entered value: `<b>{{count}}</b>`

`</template>`

We are simultaneously using the two newly created directives: `v-focus` and `v-integers-only`.

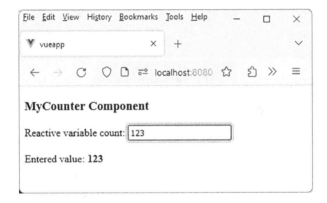

Figure 5-3. *Using the v-integers-only directive*

Only numeric characters and movement arrows are now allowed in the input field.

Step 2: Directive in the Form v-integers -only.hexa

An improvement to the `v-integers-only` directive would be to allow input of hexadecimal characters in the field. Instead of writing a new directive (with a new name, e.g., `v-integers-hexa-only`), Vue.js allows using the same directive name by associating what it calls modifiers. It is sufficient to indicate the name of the modifier used after the directive, separated by a ".".

The hexa modifier, used in the form v-integers-only.hexa, allows modifying the behavior of the v-integers-only directive to also allow hexadecimal characters in the field, in addition to the digits 0 to 9.

Let's see how to modify the v-integers-only directive to take into account the hexa modifier when used in the directive.

Each of the lifecycle methods of a directive accepts, as a second argument, the binding parameter, for example, mounted(el, binding). The binding parameter contains additional information about the directive, such as binding.modifiers, which is an object indicating the modifiers used in writing the directive.

Thus, if binding.modifiers.hexa is true, it means that the hexa modifier is used in the directive.

The v-integers-only directive is modified to account for this hexa modifier:

Considering the hexa modifier in the v-integers-only directive (file src/ directives/integers-only.js)

```
const integersOnly = {
  mounted(el, binding) {
    el.addEventListener("keydown", (event) => {
      const numbers = ["0", "1", "2", "3", "4", "5", "6", "7",
                      "8", "9"];
      const moves = ["Backspace", "ArrowLeft", "ArrowRight",
                      "Delete", "Tab", "Home", "End"];
      const letters = ["a", "b", "c", "d", "e", "f", "A", "B",
                      "C", "D", "E", "F"];

      let authorized;  // Allowed keys in the input field
```

```
    // Allow hexadecimal characters if the hexa modifier
    is present
    if (binding.modifiers.hexa) authorized = [...numbers,
    ...letters, ...moves];
    else authorized = [...numbers, ...moves];

    // If the key is not allowed, do not take it into
    account.
    // The event object is available here.
    if (!authorized.includes(event.key)) event.
    preventDefault();
  });
},
}

export default integersOnly;
```

The MyCounter component uses this new form of the directive:

**Using the v-integers-only.hexa directive (file src/components/
MyCounter.vue)**

```
<script setup>

import { ref } from "vue"

const count = ref("");

</script>

<template>

<h3>MyCounter Component</h3>

Reactive variable count: <input type="text" v-focus v-integers-
only.hexa v-model="count" />
```

```
<br/><br/>
Entered value: <b>{{count}}</b>

</template>
```

We verify that the input field now accepts hexadecimal characters in addition to the digits 0 to 9:

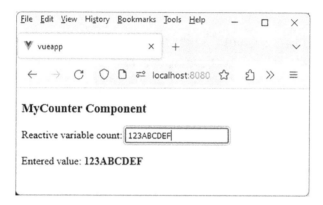

Figure 5-4. *Considering the hexa modifier in the v-integers-only directive*

Step 3: Directive in the Form v-integers-only.hexa.upper

The upper modifier allows entering characters that will be displayed in uppercase. Thus, the hexadecimal characters "a" to "f" will be transformed and displayed as "A" to "F".

Let's modify the MyCounter component to use the upper modifier.

MyCounter component with the upper modifier (file src/components/ MyCounter.vue)

```
<script setup>
```

```
import { ref } from "vue"

const count = ref("123abcDEF");

</script>

<template>

<h3>MyCounter Component</h3>

Reactive variable count: <input type="text" v-model="count"
v-focus v-integers-only.hexa.upper />
<br/><br/>
Entered value: <b>{{count}}</b>

</template>
```

Note that we positioned the v-model directive first in the input field. Indeed, directives are processed by Vue.js in the order they appear in an element. This allows, first and foremost, to initialize the content of the field with the value of the associated reactive variable, thanks to v-model. The content of the field can then be used by the following directives, which would not be possible if the v-model directive were written at the end.

The v-integers-only directive is modified to account for the upper modifier.

Considering the upper modifier in the directive (file src/directives/integers-only.js)

```
const integersOnly = {
  mounted(el, binding) {

    if (binding.modifiers.upper) {
      // Convert the displayed field to uppercase with an
      initial value
```

```
// (for this to work, the v-model directive must be
written before this one in the input field)
el.value = el.value.toUpperCase();

// Simulate an input event to mimic a keyboard keypress
// (necessary for the reactive variable linked to the
field to be updated)
el.dispatchEvent(new Event("input"));
}

el.addEventListener("keydown", (event) => {
  const numbers = ["0", "1", "2", "3", "4", "5", "6", "7",
                   "8", "9"];
  const letters = ["a", "b", "c", "d", "e", "f", "A", "B",
                   "C", "D", "E", "F"];
  const moves = ["Backspace", "ArrowLeft", "ArrowRight",
                 "Delete", "Tab", "Home", "End"];

  let authorized;  // Allowed keys in the input field

  // Allow hexadecimal characters if the hexa modifier
  is present
  if (binding.modifiers.hexa) authorized = [...numbers,
  ...letters, ...moves];
  else authorized = [...numbers, ...moves];

  // If the key is not allowed, do not take it into account
  if (!authorized.includes(event.key)) event.
  preventDefault();

  // Handle the upper modifier
  if (binding.modifiers.upper) {
    // If the key is a hexadecimal letter, convert it to
    uppercase
```

```
    if (letters.includes(event.key)) {
      const start = el.selectionStart;
      const end = el.selectionEnd;
      const text = el.value;

      // Insert the character at the cursor position
      const newText = text.substring(0, start) + event.key
      + text.substring(end);
      // Update the value of the input field (in uppercase)
      el.value = newText.toUpperCase();
      // Move the cursor after the inserted character
      el.setSelectionRange(start + 1, start + 1);

      // Prevent further processing of the key (as it has
      already been handled above)
      event.preventDefault();

      // Simulate an input event to mimic a keyboard
      keypress
      // (necessary for the reactive variable linked to the
      field to be updated)
      el.dispatchEvent(new Event("input"));
    }
  }
  });
  },
}
```

```
export default integersOnly;
```

The upper modifier complicates the writing of the directive! Indeed, we have to handle the insertion of the pressed key into the field ourselves to display it in uppercase.

Directive v-max-value Limiting the Maximum Value in an Input Field

We want to improve the management of the previous input field by limiting the value entered in the field, using a directive called v-max-value.

We will use this directive in one of the following forms:

1. v-max-value: Used in this form, the maximum value is considered to be 100. Beyond that, the input field turns red.

2. v-max-value="max": The max value refers to a max variable (reactive or not) defined in the program. If this value is exceeded, the input field turns red.

3. v-max-value.bold="max": When present in the directive, the bold modifier additionally makes the value entered in the input field bold if the max value is exceeded.

Let's see how to write these different forms of using the v-max-value directive.

Step 1: Directive in the Form v-max-value

The first form of the directive is the simplest. It assumes that the maximum value of the field is a fixed value of 100.

The MyCounter component that uses this directive is as follows:

Using the v-max-value directive (file src/components/MyCounter.vue)

```
<script setup>

import { ref } from "vue"

const count = ref("");
```

```
</script>
```

```
<template>
```

```
<h3>MyCounter Component</h3>
```

Reactive variable count: **<input type="text" v-model="count"
v-integers-only v-focus v-max-value />**
`<br/><br/>`
`Entered value: <b>{{count}}</b>`

```
</template>
```

The order of directive usage is crucial. The v-max-value directive is placed after the v-model directive: indeed, the v-model directive initializes the input field, which the v-max-value directive can then read.

The file for the v-max-value directive is src/directives/max-value.js.

v-max-value directive (file src/directives/max-value.js)

```
const maxValue = {
  mounted(el) {
    const value = el.value || 0;   // Value in the field
    if (value > 100) el.style.color = "red";
    else el.style.color = "";
  },
  updated(el) {
    const value = el.value || 0;   // Value in the field
    if (value > 100) el.style.color = "red";
    else el.style.color = "";
  },
}
```

```
export default maxValue;
```

We are utilizing the mounted() and updated() lifecycle methods. Specifically, during the mounted() phase, it is imperative to validate that the value transmitted for the input field initialization does not exceed the value of 100. This validation must also be conducted during each update of the field within the updated() method.

The procedures within these two methods are identical. Consequently, it is plausible to consolidate the processing into a function named treatment(), invoked within both mounted() and updated().

Other form of the directive (file src/directives/max-value.js)

```
const treatment = (el) => {
  const value = el.value || 0;   // Value in the field
  if (value > 100) el.style.color = "red";
  else el.style.color = "";
}

const maxValue = {
  mounted(el) {
    treatment(el);
  },
  updated(el) {
    treatment(el);
  },
}

export default maxValue;
```

The v-max-value directive is inserted into the src/directives.js file:

File src/directives.js

```
import focus from "./directives/focus";
import integersOnly from "./directives/integers-only";
import maxValue from "./directives/max-value";
```

```
export default {
  focus,
  integersOnly,
  maxValue,
}
```

Let us verify that this is functional. As soon as the input value exceeds 100, the input field should change its color to red.

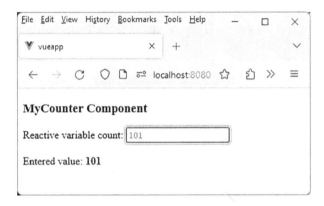

Figure 5-5. *v-max-value directive*

Step 2: Directive in the Form v-max-value="max"

Instead of setting the field's limit to a fixed value (here 100), it is also possible to transmit this value within the directive (after the "=" sign).

The max value indicated here corresponds to the value of a variable (reactive or nonreactive) initialized earlier in the program.

The MyCounter component utilizing this form of the directive becomes the following:

MyCounter component (file src/components/MyCounter.vue)

```
<script setup>

import { ref } from "vue"

const count = ref("201");
const max = 200;

</script>

<template>

<h3>MyCounter Component</h3>

Reactive variable count: <input type="text" v-model="count"
v-integers-only v-focus v-max-value="max" />
<br/><br/>
Max value: <b>{{max}}</b>
<br/><br/>
Entered value: <b>{{count}}</b>

</template>
```

The maximum value of the field is initialized here to the value of 200. The v-max-value directive is modified to handle the value assigned to it.

v-max-value directive (file src/directives/max-value.js)

```
const treatment = (el, binding) => {
  const maxValue = binding.value || 100;  // 100 by default
  const value = el.value || 0;  // Value in the field
  if (value > maxValue) el.style.color = "red";
  else el.style.color = "";
}
```

```
const maxValue = {
  mounted(el, binding) {
    treatment(el, binding);
  },
  updated(el, binding) {
    treatment(el, binding);
  },
}
```

```
export default maxValue;
```

The value assigned to the directive in the template is retrieved using binding.value. If the value is not specified, it defaults to 100 as before.

The input field will turn red as soon as the value of 200 is exceeded in the input field (here, when it reaches 201):

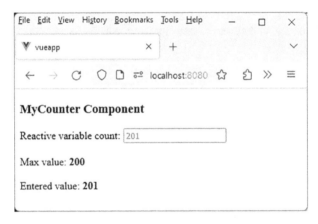

Figure 5-6. *v-max-value="max" Directive*

Step 3: Directive in the Form v-max-value. bold="max"

This form of the directive is similar to the previous one, but we integrate the bold modifier, which changes the appearance of the input field (making it bold) when the field value exceeds the maximum allowed value:

- If the bold modifier is absent from the directive, the behavior is similar to that of the previous example.

- If the bold modifier is present in the directive, the input field is made bold when the maximum value is exceeded. The previous behavior of the directive is also retained (the input field turns red if the value is exceeded).

Let's see how to use this new form of the directive in the MyCounter component:

MyCounter component (file src/components/MyCounter.vue)

```
<script setup>

import { ref } from "vue"

const count = ref("201");
const max = 200;

</script>

<template>

<h3>MyCounter Component</h3>

Reactive variable count: <input type="text" v-model="count"
v-integers-only v-focus v-max-value.bold="max" />
<br/><br/>
```

```
Max value: <b>{{max}}</b>
<br/><br/>
Entered value: <b>{{count}}</b>
```

```
</template>
```

The directive is modified to incorporate the consideration of the bold modifier:

Bold modifier in the v-max-value directive (file src/directives/max-value.js)

```
const treatment = (el, binding) => {
  const maxValue = binding.value || 100;  // 100 by default
  const value = el.value || 0;  // Value in the field
  const bold = binding.modifiers.bold;
  if (value > maxValue) {
    el.style.color = "red";
    if (bold) {
      el.style.fontWeight = "bold";
      el.style.fontFamily = "arial";
    }
  }
  else {
    el.style.color = "";
    el.style.fontWeight = "";  // Removal of "bold"
    el.style.fontFamily = "";  // Removal of "arial"
  }
}

const maxValue = {
  mounted(el, binding) {
    treatment(el, binding);
  },
```

```
updated(el, binding) {
    treatment(el, binding);
  },
}
```

```
export default maxValue;
```

When the maximum value is exceeded, we set the font to "bold" and also modify it to "Arial" to make the change even more noticeable on the screen.

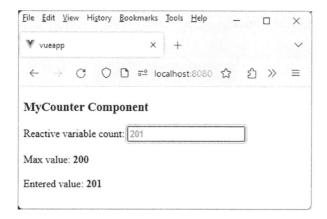

Figure 5-7. *Utilization of the "bold" modifier in the directive*

The maximum value of 200 having been exceeded, the input field has turned red and bold.

v-focus Directive for Giving Focus

We have previously created this directive in the preceding pages, using it in the form v-focus. We will use the v-focus directive in one of the following forms:

1. `v-focus`: This simplest form of the directive gives focus to the input field on which the directive is applied. We have used this form previously.

2. `v-focus:color="color"`: This form of the directive allows specifying a value for the `color` argument of the directive. The input field gains focus, and the text color becomes the one indicated in the `color` variable.

3. `v-focus:backcolor="bcolor"`: This form of the directive allows indicating a value for the `backcolor` argument of the directive. The input field gains focus, and the background color of the text becomes the one indicated in the `bcolor` variable.

4. `v-focus:colors="colors"`: This form of the directive allows specifying in the `colors` variable, in the form `{ color, backgroundcolor }`, the text and background colors of the input field when it gains focus.

To enable us to learn additional aspects of directives, we wish to explain here the use of arguments in directives.

Step 1: What Is an Argument in a Directive?

An argument is used after the directive's name, separated by the ":" symbol. For example, we write `v-focus:color="'blue'"`, to indicate that the text color should be blue when the element has focus.

In this case, we say that the `v-focus` directive has an argument named `color`, with its value set to `"blue"`.

What is the difference between "'blue'" and "blue"? Note that here we specify the value as "'blue'" and not just "blue". Indeed, if we write it as "blue", it refers to a variable (reactive or nonreactive) named blue, while we intend to assign the string "blue", hence the notation "'blue'". What is written within the string "" must be a JavaScript expression, which is the case with 'blue'.

Why use an argument in a directive? One might think that we could simply write the directive as v-focus="'blue'". However, this is less precise than writing v-focus:color="'blue'" because we might also want to write v-focus:backgroundcolor="'yellow'" to change the background color in that case.

The argument's name (color, backgroundcolor) helps specify the type of value indicated in the directive, especially when multiple types of values are possible (color, backgroundcolor).

What is the difference between a modifier and an argument? A modifier specifies a behavior in a directive, while an argument provides a value (for that argument). We use an argument to indicate a value and a modifier to specify a specific behavior (making it bold, uppercase, etc.).

Is an argument necessary? If the directive's value type is unique (e.g., always a maximum value, a color, etc.), there is no need to use an argument. In this case, it suffices to indicate a value to the directive without specifying the argument to which the value corresponds. The argument in a directive serves only to specify what the value corresponds to (color, backgroundcolor).

Now that we have clarified that, let's use this information to enhance the v-focus directive with new functionalities.

Step 2: Directive in the Form v-focus

This form of the directive is the one we previously wrote. We rewrite it here to show how it will evolve based on the arguments used later.

The MyCounter component uses the v-focus directive:

Utilization of the v-focus directive in the MyCounter component (file src/components/MyCounter.vue)

```
<script setup>

import { ref } from "vue"

const count = ref("12345");

</script>

<template>

<h3>MyCounter Component</h3>

Reactive variable count: <input type="text" v-model="count"
          v-focus />
<br/><br/>
Entered value: <b>{{count}}</b>

</template>
```

The v-focus directive is described as follows:

v-focus directive (file src/directives/focus.js)

```
const focusDirective = {
  mounted(el) {
    el.focus();
  },
};

export default focusDirective;
```

When the MyCounter component is displayed, the input field immediately gains focus.

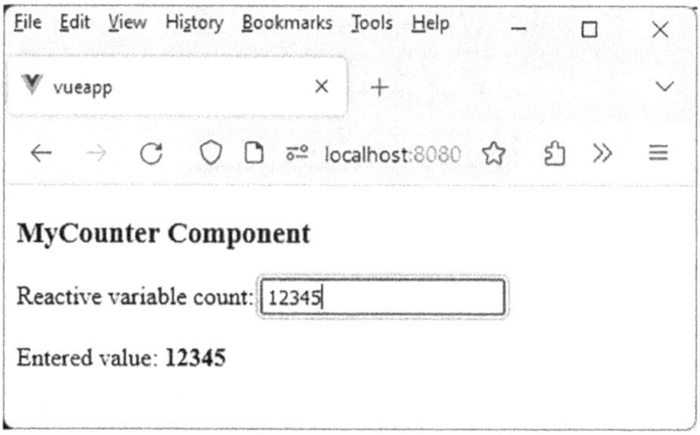

Figure 5-8. *The input field gains focus*

Step 3: Directive in the Form v-focus:color="color"

This form of the directive allows specifying a value for the directive. As this value is a color, an additional `color` argument is used to specify the type of the value. Later, we will see that we can also use the arguments `backgroundcolor` and `colors` to indicate other types of values, hence the use of arguments to specify the type of value used.

The `MyCounter` component using this form of the directive is as follows:

MyCounter component (file src/components/MyCounter.vue)

```
<script setup>

import { ref } from "vue"

const count = ref("12345");
const color = "cyan";

</script>

<template>
```

```
<h3>MyCounter Component</h3>
```

Reactive variable count: **`<input type="text" v-model="count"`**
       `v-focus:color="color" />`
```
<br/><br/>
Entered value: <b>{{count}}</b>
```

```
</template>
```

The directive is specified here in the form `v-focus:color="color"` because `color` is a variable defined in the program. If we were to directly specify a value in the directive (without using a variable name), we would write it in the form `v-focus:color="'cyan'"` as explained earlier.

The directive file is modified to accommodate this new argument:

v-focus directive with the color argument (file src/directives/focus.js)

```
const focusDirective = {
  mounted(el, binding) {
    el.focus();
    const arg = binding.arg;
    const value = binding.value;
    if (arg == "color") el.style.color = value;
  }
};
```

```
export default focusDirective;
```

The input field gains focus, and the input field's color changes to "cyan".

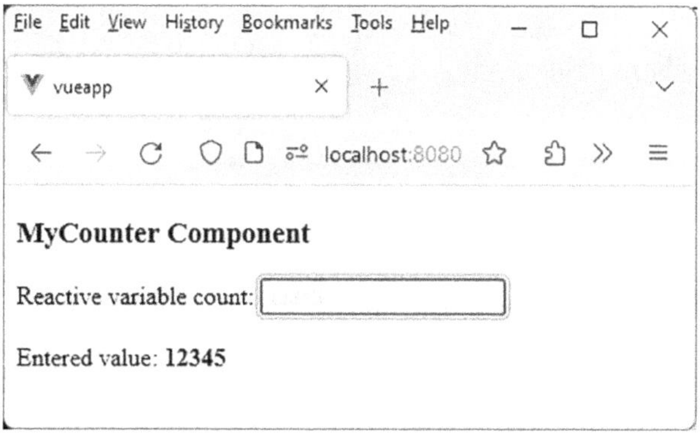

Figure 5-9. *Input field with focus and cyan color*

Note in this example that the input field retains its new color even if the input field loses focus. It would be necessary to restore the previous color of the input field when it loses focus.

To achieve this, we need to handle the focus and blur events on the input field. Let's modify the directive for that purpose.

Handling the focus and blur events in the v-focus directive (file src/ directives/focus.js)

```
const focusDirective = {
  mounted(el, binding) {
    const arg = binding.arg;
    const value = binding.value;
    // Position the handling of the focus and blur events
    el.addEventListener("focus", () => {
      if (arg == "color") el.style.color = value;
    });
    el.addEventListener("blur", () => {
      if (arg == "color") el.style.color = "";
```

```
  });
  // and then give focus to the input field
  el.focus();
  }
};
```

```
export default focusDirective;
```

We modify the color of the input field upon entering the field (focus event) and then restore the initial color upon leaving the field (blur event). Additionally, we give focus to the input field only after positioning the event handlers; otherwise, they would not be considered during the initial display of the component.

Let's verify that this is functional. Upon launching the program, the input field gains focus, and the color of the input field is modified:

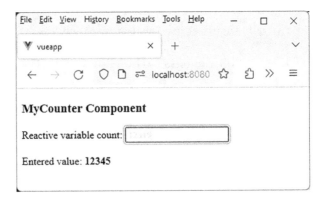

Figure 5-10. *Gaining focus in the input field*

Then click outside the input field. The color of the input field is removed.

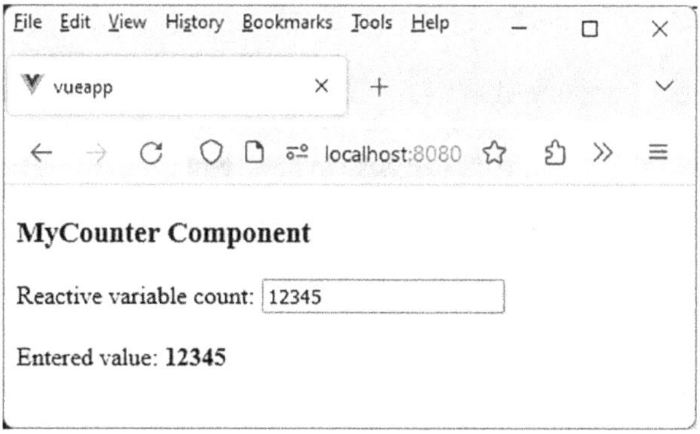

Figure 5-11. *The input field has lost focus*

This form of the v-focus directive, using the focus and blur events, will be retained in the following examples.

Step 4: Directive in the Form v-focus:backgroundcolor="bcolor"

Another form of the v-focus directive uses the backgroundcolor argument to specify a background color in the directive.

The modifications to the MyCounter component and the directive are similar to those previously made to use the color argument.

The MyCounter component using the backgroundcolor argument in the v-focus directive becomes the following:

MyCounter component (file src/components/MyCounter.vue)

```
<script setup>

import { ref } from "vue"

const count = ref("12345");
const color = "cyan";

</script>
```

```
<template>

<h3>MyCounter Component</h3>

Reactive variable count: <input type="text" v-model="count"
          v-focus:backgroundcolor="color" />
<br/><br/>
Entered value: <b>{{count}}</b>

</template>
```

The v-focus directive implementing the backgroundcolor argument becomes the following:

v-focus directive using the backgroundcolor argument (file src/directives/focus.js)

```
const focusDirective = {
  mounted(el, binding) {
    const arg = binding.arg;
    const value = binding.value;
    // Position the handling of the focus and blur events
    el.addEventListener("focus", () => {
      if (arg == "color") el.style.color = value;
      if (arg == "backgroundcolor") el.style.backgroundColor
      = value;
    });
    el.addEventListener("blur", () => {
      if (arg == "color") el.style.color = "";
      if (arg == "backgroundcolor") el.style.
      backgroundColor = "";
    });
```

```
  // and then give focus to the input field
  el.focus();
 }
};

export default focusDirective;
```

We have simply added the handling of the `backgroundcolor` argument in a similar fashion to that of the `color` argument.

The `MyCounter` component is now displayed:

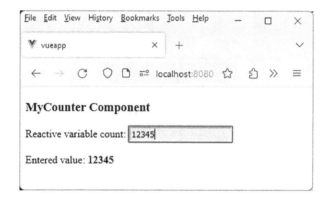

Figure 5-12. *Utilization of the backgroundcolor argument in the v-focus directive*

Step 5: Directive in the Form v-focus:colors="colors"

The `v-focus` directive now has both the `color` and `backgroundcolor` arguments. However, only one of the two can be specified when using the directive.

Hence, the creation of the new `colors` argument, which allows specifying the values of both arguments in the form of an object `{ color, backgroundcolor }`.

The MyCounter component becomes the following:

MyCounter component (file src/components/MyCounter.vue)

```
<script setup>

import { ref } from "vue"

const count = ref("12345");
const colors = { color:"cyan", backgroundcolor:"black" };

</script>

<template>

<h3>MyCounter Component</h3>

Reactive variable count: <input type="text" v-model="count"
          v-focus:colors="colors" />
<br/><br/>
Entered value: <b>{{count}}</b>

</template>
```

The v-focus directive is modified to use this new argument, in addition to the two others:

v-focus directive (file src/directives/focus.js)

```
const focusDirective = {
  mounted(el, binding) {
    const arg = binding.arg;
    const value = binding.value;
    // Position the handling of the focus and blur events
    el.addEventListener("focus", () => {
      if (arg == "color") el.style.color = value;
```

```
    if (arg == "backgroundcolor") el.style.backgroundColor
    = value;
    if (arg == "colors") {
      el.style.color = value.color;
      el.style.backgroundColor = value.backgroundcolor;
    }
  });
  el.addEventListener("blur", () => {
    if (arg == "color") el.style.color = "";
    if (arg == "backgroundcolor") el.style.
    backgroundColor = "";
    if (arg == "colors") {
      el.style.color = "";
      el.style.backgroundColor = "";
    }
  });
  // and then give focus to the input field
  el.focus();
  }
};

export default focusDirective;
```

The MyCounter component now takes into account a new text and background color for the input field:

Figure 5-13. *Utilization of the colors argument in the v-focus directive*

v-clearable Directive for Adding a Clear Button to the Input Field

Let's now demonstrate a new directive that adds a Clear button after an input field, allowing the user to clear the input field's content. The v-clearable directive inserts the button directly after the input field.

The MyCounter component using the directive would be as follows:

MyCounter component using the v-clearable directive (file src/ components/MyCounter.vue)

```
<script setup>

import { ref } from "vue"

const count = ref("Text to be cleared");

</script>

<template>

<h3>MyCounter Component</h3>
```

```
Reactive variable count: <input type="text" v-model="count"
        v-clearable v-focus />
<br/><br/>
Entered value: <b>{{count}}</b>

</template>
```

We display an input field with the v-clearable directive in the template. When the directive v-clearable will be written, the component will appear as follows:

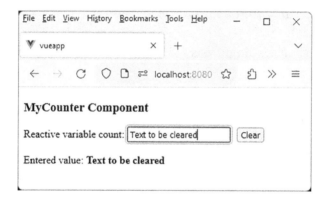

Figure 5-14. *Input field with a Clear button*

Clicking the Clear button clears the content of the input field:

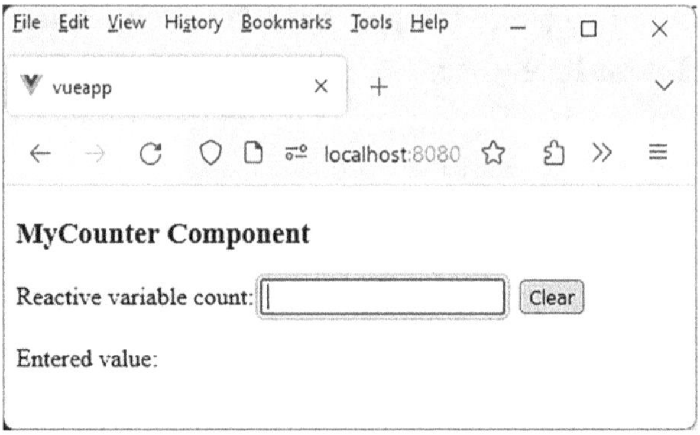

Figure 5-15. *The input field has been cleared*

The v-clearable directive is written in the file src/directives/
clearable.js:

v-clearable directive (file src/directives/clearable.js)

```
const clearable = {
  mounted(el) {
    const clearButton = document.createElement("button");
    clearButton.innerHTML = "Clear";
    clearButton.style = "position:relative; left:10px;";

    // Handle the click on the button (clear the content of the
    input field).
    clearButton.addEventListener("click", () => {
      // Clear the content of the input field.
      el.value = "";
      // Simulate an input event to mimic a keyboard key press
      // (mandatory to ensure that the reactive variable linked
      to the input field is updated)
      el.dispatchEvent(new Event("input"));
      // Give focus to the input field
      el.focus();
```

```
  });

  // Insert the button after the input field
  el.parentNode.insertBefore(clearButton, el.nextSibling);
  }
};

export default clearable;
```

The v-clearable directive is then inserted into the file src/directives.js:

File src/directives.js

```
import focus from "./directives/focus";
import integersOnly from "./directives/integers-only";
import maxValue from "./directives/max-value";
import clearable from "./directives/clearable";

export default {
  focus,
  integersOnly,
  maxValue,
  clearable,
}
```

The v-clearable directive is now ready for being used.

v-timer Directive for Displaying Real-Time Clock

The v-timer directive replaces the content of the element it is applied to with the current time in the format HH:MM:SS. It has several derived forms:

1.   v-timer: This is the simplest form of the directive. It displays the current time in real time, in the format HH:MM:SS.

2.   v-timer.ms: The ms modifier of the directive allows displaying tenths of a second after the seconds.

3.   v-timer.chrono: The chrono modifier starts a stopwatch in the format HH:MM:SS starting from 00:00:00. It increments every second, or every tenth of a second if the ms modifier is present.

Let's see how to implement these different forms of the v-timer directive.

Step 1: Directive in the Form v-timer

The MyCounter component using this directive can be written as follows:

Utilization of the v-timer directive (file src/components/ MyCounter.vue)

```
<script setup>

</script>

<template>

<h3>MyCounter Component</h3>
```

It is <span v-timer />

```
</template>
```

The content of the <span v-timer> element will be replaced by the current time in the format HH:MM:SS.

The v-timer directive is created in the file src/directives/timer.js:

v-timer directive (file src/directives/timer.js)

```
const timer = {
  mounted(el) {
    // Initialization of the displayed time
    // (allows it to be displayed immediately without waiting
    for a second)
    let time = getCurrentTime();
    el.innerHTML = time;
    setInterval(()=>{
      // Then incrementing the time every second
      let time = getCurrentTime();
      el.innerHTML = time;
    }, 1000);  // Every 1000 milliseconds (1 second).
  },
}

function getCurrentTime() {
  // Return the current time in the format HH:MM:SS
  const now = new Date();
  const hours = now.getHours().toString().padStart(2, '0');
  const minutes = now.getMinutes().toString().padStart(2, '0');
  const seconds = now.getSeconds().toString().padStart(2, '0');
  return `${hours}:${minutes}:${seconds}`;
}

export default timer;
```

The getCurrentTime() method returns the current time in the format HH:MM:SS. This time is then displayed in the el element using the v-timer directive. The setInterval(callback) method, with the processing function called every second (1000 milliseconds), refreshes the displayed time.

253

To function, the directive must be included in the src/directives.
js file:

Insertion of the directive (file src/directives.js)

```
import focus from "./directives/focus";
import integersOnly from "./directives/integers-only";
import maxValue from "./directives/max-value";
import clearable from "./directives/clearable";
import timer from "./directives/timer";

export default {
  focus,
  integersOnly,
  maxValue,
  clearable,
  timer,
}
```

Let's verify that the time is incremented every second:

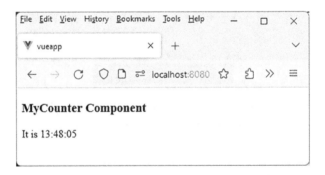

Figure 5-16. *Displaying the time with the v-timer directive*

Step 2: Directive in the Form v-timer.ms

Another form of the directive allows for more precision by also displaying tenths of a second. For this, the ms modifier is used following the v-timer directive.

The v-timer directive is modified:

Using the ms modifier in the v-timer directive (file src/directives/ timer.js)

```
const timer = {
  mounted(el, binding) {
    const ms = binding.modifiers.ms;
    let time = getCurrentTime(ms);
    el.innerHTML = time;
    setInterval(()=>{
      let time = getCurrentTime(ms);
      el.innerHTML = time;
    }, 100);
  },
}

function getCurrentTime(ms = false) {
  const now = new Date();
  const hours = now.getHours().toString().padStart(2, '0');
  const minutes = now.getMinutes().toString().padStart(2, '0');
  const seconds = now.getSeconds().toString().padStart(2, '0');
  let formattedTime = `${hours}:${minutes}:${seconds}`;

  if (ms) {
    const milliseconds = now.getMilliseconds().toString().
    slice(0, 1); // Obtaining tenths of a second
    formattedTime += `.${milliseconds}`;
  }
```

```
  return formattedTime;
}
```

```
export default timer;
```

The getCurrentTime() function is modified to consider the optional ms parameter, indicating to format the time by adding tenths of a second at the end. The ms modifier is taken into account in the v-timer directive, through binding.modifiers.ms, which is true if the ms modifier is present, false otherwise.

Let's use both forms of the v-timer directive in the MyCounter component:

MyCounter component (file src/components/MyCounter.vue)

```
<script setup>

</script>

<template>

<h3>MyCounter Component</h3>

It is <span v-timer />
<br>
It is <span v-timer.ms /> more precisely

</template>
```

The displayed result is as follows:

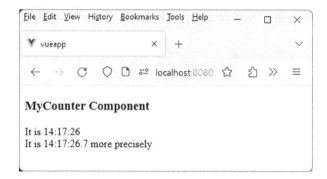

Figure 5-17. *Using both forms of the v-timer directive*

The first timer displays the time every second, while the second displays the time every tenth of a second.

Step 3: Directive in the Form v-timer.chrono

The chrono modifier in the v-timer directive allows immediately starting a stopwatch.

The MyCounter component file is modified to display it:

Display a stopwatch (file src/components/MyCounter.vue)

```
<script setup>

</script>

<template>

<h3>MyCounter Component</h3>

It is <span v-timer />
<br>
It is <span v-timer.ms /> more precisely
<br>
<br>
```

```
Elapsed time <span v-timer.chrono />
<br>
Elapsed time <span v-timer.chrono.ms />   more precisely

</template>
```

The ms modifier can be used with the chrono modifier to add more precision to the elapsed time. The processing of the chrono modifier is inserted into the v-timer directive file:

Using the chrono modifier in the v-timer directive (file src/directives/ timer.js)

```
const timer = {
  mounted(el, binding) {
    const ms = binding.modifiers.ms;
    const chrono = binding.modifiers.chrono;

    // Initialization of the clock or stopwatch.
    if (!chrono) {
      let time = getCurrentTime(ms);
      el.innerHTML = time;
    }
    else {
      if (!ms) el.innerHTML = "00:00:00";
      else el.innerHTML = "00:00:00.0";
    }

    setInterval(()=>{
      if (!chrono) {
        let time = getCurrentTime(ms);
        el.innerHTML = time;
      }
      else {
        const chronoTime = getChronoTime(ms);
```

```
      el.innerHTML = chronoTime;
    }
  }, 100);
 },
}

function getCurrentTime(ms = false) {
  const now = new Date();
  const hours = now.getHours().toString().padStart(2, '0');
  const minutes = now.getMinutes().toString().padStart(2, '0');
  const seconds = now.getSeconds().toString().padStart(2, '0');
  let formattedTime = `${hours}:${minutes}:${seconds}`;

  if (ms) {
    const milliseconds = now.getMilliseconds().toString().
    slice(0, 1); // Obtaining tenths of a second
    formattedTime += `.${milliseconds}`;
  }

  return formattedTime;
}

let startChronoTime = new Date();  // Starting time of the
stopwatch

function getChronoTime(ms = false) {
  const now = new Date();
  const elapsedMilliseconds = now.getTime() - startChronoTime.
  getTime();

  const hours = Math.floor(elapsedMilliseconds / (3600
  * 1000));
  const remainingMilliseconds1 = elapsedMilliseconds % (3600
  * 1000);
```

```
const minutes = Math.floor(remainingMilliseconds1 / (60
* 1000));
const remainingMilliseconds2 = remainingMilliseconds1 % (60
* 1000);

const seconds = Math.floor(remainingMilliseconds2 / 1000);

let formattedTime = `${hours.toString().padStart(2,
'0')}:${minutes.toString().padStart(2, '0')}:${seconds.
toString().padStart(2, '0')}`;

if (ms) {
  const milliseconds = Math.floor(remainingMilliseconds2
  % 1000);
  const tenthsOfSecond = Math.floor((milliseconds %
  1000) / 100);
  formattedTime += `.${tenthsOfSecond.toString()}`;
}

  return formattedTime;
}

export default timer;
```

Following the same principle as the getCurrentTime() function, we create the getChronoTime() function, which allows retrieving the elapsed time in the format HH:MM:SS. After a certain time, the display becomes the following:

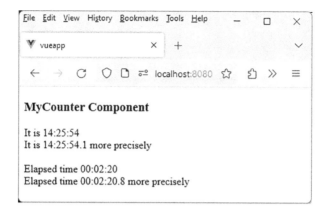

Figure 5-18. *Displays of the v-timer directive*

Conclusion

We have explained how to create new directives in Vue.js, simplifying the code of our Vue.js components. Thanks to arguments and modifiers, Vue.js directives offer incredible functionalities that allow simple and intuitive use in components.

CHAPTER 6

Day 6: Mastering the Creation of Composables in Vue.js

As seen in the previous chapter, creating new directives makes it easier to manipulate the HTML elements on which the directives are used. In this chapter, we will explore composables. Composables are also known as composition functions.

Composables defined in our Vue.js components are used to encapsulate application logic in the form of reusable functions. Thus, they are oriented toward internal component logic and data management.

Why Create Composables?

Creating composables in a Vue.js application is useful for several reasons, as described in the following:

© Eric Sarrion 2024
E. Sarrion, *Master Vue.js in 6 Days*, https://doi.org/10.1007/979-8-8688-0364-2_6

1. **Reusability of Code**: Composables allow grouping functionalities into reusable modules. This means writing the functionality once and using it in multiple components of the application without repeating it.

2. **State Management**: Composables are particularly useful for managing the application state. State management is encapsulated in a composition function, making data management more consistent and predictable. It also facilitates handling the global state of the application.

3. **Ease of Testing**: Composables are easy to test in isolation.

4. **Scalability**: Composables promote the scalability of the application. New features can be added or existing logic modified in a composition function without having to modify many components.

Composables are a powerful tool for improving the structure, maintainability, and code reuse in Vue.js.

Differences Between Composables and Directives

Creating composables allows us to write Vue.js component code better, much like directives also allow. However, directives and composables are not used in the same way.

Directives help write HTML code within the `<template>` section of components, simplifying this code to the maximum.

Composables help write JavaScript code within the `<script setup>` section of the component, allowing the use of functionalities defined in the functions called composables.

Therefore, with the ability to write new directives and create composables, Vue.js enables us to write the entire code that creates Vue.js components more effectively.

Creating a Vue.js Composable

A Vue.js composable is a JavaScript function. Like any function, it may have optional input parameters and may return a result.

A composable is meant to provide a service. We create a composable when we have identified a service to provide in our component. This service may also be used in other components, making our composable even more useful.

Because a composable is meant to provide a service, it is customary to start its name with the word `"use"`, followed by the name given to the composable.

For example:

1. `useCounter()`: This composable manages actions in a component like `MyCounter` (incrementing, decrementing the counter).

2. `useFetch()`: This composable performs an HTTP request and retrieves information from a remote server.

Thus, to create a composable, you must first ask the following questions:

1. What are its parameters?

2. What data or functionalities does it return?

265

These questions help identify the parameters and return of the JavaScript function associated with the composable. These are the questions to ask whenever you want to create a new composable.

As a composable can be used in several components, tradition dictates grouping composables in the `composables` directory within the `src` directory.

Let's see, with a simple example, how to create the `useCounter()` composable to manage the `MyCounter` component.

Step 1: Creating the useCounter( ) Composable

The `useCounter()` composable manages the increment and decrement of the counter associated with the `MyCounter` component.

Without using composables, the `MyCounter` component we wrote in Chapter 1 was as follows:

MyCounter component (file src/components/MyCounter.vue)

```
<script setup>

import { ref } from 'vue';

const count = ref(0);

const increment = () => {
  count.value++;
}

const decrement = () => {
  count.value--;
}

</script>
```

```
<template>

<h3>MyCounter Component</h3>
Reactive variable count : <b>{{ count }}</b>
<br /><br />
<button @click="increment">count+1</button>
 
<button @click="decrement">count-1</button>

</template>
```

The increment() and decrement() functions of the counter are defined in the <script setup> section of the component. They are then used in the <template> section of the component.

The idea behind composables is to externalize data management into external functions called composables. These composable functions will then be available and used in components that require them.

In the case of the MyCounter component, we externalize the management of the count variable, including its increment and decrement, into a composable named useCounter().

Let's examine the parameters and possible returns of the useCounter() composable. Thus, the useCounter() composable:

1. Will have an init parameter, which is the initialization value of the counter.

2. Will return as data the current value count of the counter (managed within the composable, hence made available as a return value), and the functions increment() and decrement() allowing to increment or decrement the counter value. These elements will be accessible in the component that uses this composable.

Usage of the useCounter() composable in the MyCounter component (file src/components/MyCounter.vue)

```
<script setup>

import useCounter from "../composables/useCounter.js"

const [count, increment, decrement] = useCounter(0);  // 0 =
Initialization of the counter

</script>

<template>

<h3>MyCounter Component</h3>
Reactive variable count : <b>{{ count }}</b>
<br /><br />
<button @click="increment">count+1</button>
 
<button @click="decrement">count-1</button>

</template>
```

The `<script setup>` section of the `MyCounter` component has now become simpler, thanks to the use of the `useCounter()` composable:

1. The `useCounter()` composable is first imported into the component.

2. The `useCounter(0)` function of the composable is called with the initialization value 0 and returns, in the form of an array, the values [count, increment, decrement], which, respectively, correspond to the current value of the counter and the `increment()` and `decrement()` functions of the counter.

The count variable is then used in the template of the component, as well as the increment() and decrement() functions, which are called when clicking the "count+1" or "count-1" button of the component.

The useCounter() composable is created in the useCounter.js file in the src/composables directory. It is written as follows:

useCounter() composable (file src/composables/useCounter.js)

```
import { ref } from "vue";

const useCounter = (init) => {
  const count = ref(init);
  const increment = () => {
    count.value++;
  }
  const decrement = () => {
    count.value--;
  }
  return [count, increment, decrement];
}

export default useCounter;
```

It is evident that the complete management of the reactive variable count is integrated into the composable, which streamlines the code of the MyCounter component.

Let us verify that the component functions:

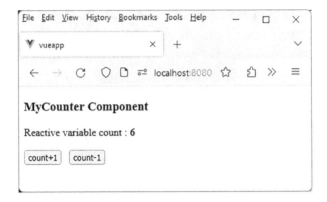

Figure 6-1. *useCounter() composable*

Step 2: Return Composable Data As an Array or As an Object?

In the previous example, we observed that the useCounter() composable returns an array [count, increment, decrement]. Alternatively, we could have returned an object {count, increment, decrement}.

Usage As an Array

If we use return [count, increment, decrement] in the composable, we dictate the order of the elements returned in the array. They must then be used in the same order, but not necessarily under the same names, in the component using the composable.

Thus, in the MyCounter component, we could write the following:

```
const [count1, increment1, decrement1] = useCounter(0);
```

Then, the count1 variable and the increment1() and decrement1() functions can be used in the component.

Moreover, if an element returned by the composable is not used in the component, it can be written as follows:

If the MyCounter component does not use the increment() function returned by the composable:

```
const [count, , decrement] = useCounter(0);  // increment is
not used
```

Usage As an Object

If we use return {count, increment, decrement} in the composable, the names used in the returned object cannot be changed during their usage. However, the order of properties in the object no longer matters.

Thus, in the MyCounter component, we could write the following:

```
const {decrement, increment, count} = useCounter(0);
```

The order of the returned elements is changed, but not their names because the names of object properties are not modifiable, while their order of appearance does not matter. Therefore, an object {key1, key2} is equivalent to an object {key2, key1}.

Thus, a composable can return data as an array or as an object, with the constraints mentioned previously. However, in the examples that follow, it will be seen that it is more judicious to return data as an array rather than as an object.

Improving a Vue.js Composable

We will now see how, based on a previous composable, it is possible to enhance it to provide new functionalities.

We will start with the useCounter() composable and create two new composables that will be used in the MyCounter component. These are the following composables:

1. useCounterMax(): This composable allows setting a maximum value for the counter, not to be exceeded.

2. useCounterMaxWithError(): This composable is similar to the previous one but also displays an error message if attempting to exceed the maximum value.

Let's start by creating the useCounterMax() composable.

Step 1: useCounterMax( ) Composable

This composable is used in the form useCounterMax(init, max) and allows blocking the incrementation of the counter when it reaches a maximum value indicated in the parameters.

The MyCounter component using this composable is written as follows:

Usage of the useCounterMax() composable in the MyCounter component (file src/components/MyCounter.vue)

```
<script setup>

import useCounterMax from "../composables/useCounterMax"

const init = 1;
const max = 5;
const [count, increment, decrement] = useCounterMax(init, max);

</script>

<template>

<h3>MyCounter Component</h3>
Reactive variable count: <b>{{ count }}</b>
<br><br>
Maximum value: <b>{{max}}</b>
```

```
<br /><br />
<button @click="increment">count+1</button>
 
<button @click="decrement">count-1</button>

</template>
```

The code of the MyCounter component is almost identical to the previous one. We have only imported the new useCounterMax() composable, and we display the maximum value not to exceed in the template.

The useCounterMax() composable returns the same information as the previous useCounter() composable:

- The count variable corresponds to the value of the reactive variable.

- The increment() function increments the variable if possible (i.e., if the maximum value is not reached).

- The decrement() function decrements the variable.

Let's write the new useCounterMax(init, max) composable. It utilizes the previously written useCounter(init) composable.

**useCounterMax() composable (file src/composables/
useCounterMax.js)**

```
import useCounter from "../composables/useCounter";

const useCounterMax = (init, max) => {
  const [count, increment, decrement] = useCounter(init);
  const incrementMax = () => {
    if (count.value >= max) {
      return;  // Avoid incrementing
    }
    else {
```

273

```
        increment();  // Increment
    }
  }
  return [count, incrementMax, decrement];
}

export default useCounterMax;
```

The new useCounterMax() composable uses the old useCounter() composable. Only the increment() function is modified, named incrementMax() here to differentiate it. If the maximum value is reached, we do not increment; otherwise, we increment by calling the old increment() function available in the old useCounter() composable.

Because we return the composable data as an array, it is sufficient to respect the order of the returned data in the new composable, even if their names are different. Thus, we return incrementMax(), but you can use the name increment() in the component using it, which avoids modifying the MyCounter component (outside of the name of the used composable).

Let's verify that this works:

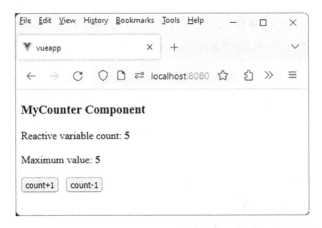

Figure 6-2. *Usage of the useCounterMax() composable*

The counter is blocked at the maximum value, which cannot be exceeded.

274

Step 2: useCounterMaxWithError( ) Composable

Let's enhance the useCounterMax() composable by allowing it to display an error message if attempting to exceed the maximum value.

This will be the role of the new useCounterMaxWithError() composable, which displays an error message in this case.

- The input parameters are init and max.

- The returned data is an array [count, increment, decrement, error], where error corresponds to a reactive variable that will display the error message.

The MyCounter component is now written as follows:

Usage of the useCounterMaxWithError composable (file src/components/MyCounter.vue)

```
<script setup>

import useCounterMaxWithError from "../composables/
useCounterMaxWithError"

const init = 1;
const max = 5;
const [count, increment, decrement, error] =
useCounterMaxWithError(init, max);

</script>

<template>

<h3>MyCounter Component</h3>
Reactive variable count: <b>{{ count }}</b>
<br><br>
Maximum value: <b>{{max}}</b>
```

```
<br><br>
```
Error: {{error}}

```
<br /><br />
<button @click="increment">count+1</button>
 
<button @click="decrement">count-1</button>

</template>
```

The useCounterMaxWithError() composable is written as follows:

useCounterMaxWithError() composable (file src/composables/
useCounterMaxWithError.js)

```
import useCounter from "../composables/useCounter";
import { ref } from "vue";

const useCounterMaxWithError = (init, max) => {
  const [count, increment, decrement] = useCounter(init);
  const error = ref("");
  const incrementMax = () => {
    if (count.value >= max) {
      error.value = "Maximum value reached!";
    }
    else {
      increment();
      error.value = "";
    }
  }
  const decrementMax = () => {
    decrement();
    if (count.value <= max) {
      error.value = "";
    }
```

```
}
  return [count, incrementMax, decrementMax, error];
}

export default useCounterMaxWithError;
```

Using a reactive variable, defined as const error = ref(""), is essential for displaying the error message because it allows for reactivity in the user interface. Vue.js leverages reactivity to efficiently update the DOM when the underlying data changes. When a simple variable is used (e.g., let error), changes to that variable within the program may not be reflected on the screen.

Let's verify that this works:

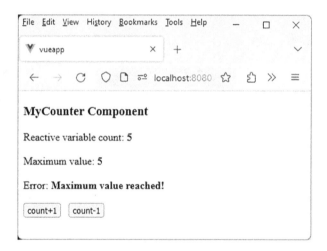

Figure 6-3. *Display of the error message in the composable*

As soon as the max value is exceeded, the error is displayed.

Step 3: Improved useCounterMaxWithError () Composable

The previous composable functions correctly. However, if the initial value is set to a value higher than the max value, no error message is displayed.

Let's write these values into the MyCounter component:

Initialization (file src/components/MyCounter.vue)

```
const init = 10;
const max = 5;  // init > max
```

This displays the following result:

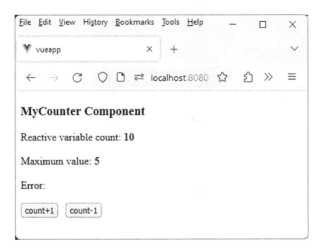

Figure 6-4. *Initial counter value higher than the maximum value: no error displayed*

To remedy this, the composable should test the values passed by the component during its initialization. A composable has access to all the functionalities of a component, particularly its lifecycle through methods such as onMounted(), onUpdated(), etc. These are the lifecycle methods of a Vue.js component that were described in Chapter 1.

Let's use the onMounted() method, which allows for processing when the component is mounted in the DOM.

The useCounterMaxWithError() composable becomes the following:

Utilization of the onMounted() method in the composable (file src/composables/useCounterMaxWithError.js)

```
import useCounter from "../composables/useCounter";
import { ref, onMounted } from "vue";

const useCounterMaxWithError = (init, max) => {
  const [count, increment, decrement] = useCounter(init);
  const error = ref("");
  const incrementMax = () => {
    if (count.value >= max) {
      error.value = "Maximum value reached!";
    }
    else {
      increment();
      error.value = "";
    }
  }
  const decrementMax = () => {
    decrement();
    if (count.value <= max) {
      error.value = "";
    }
  }
  onMounted(()=> {
    if (count.value > max) error.value = "Maximum value
    reached!";
  });
```

```
  return [count, incrementMax, decrementMax, error];
}

export default useCounterMaxWithError;
```

Let us verify that the error is now displayed when the initial value of the counter exceeds the maximum value:

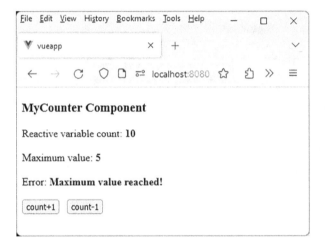

Figure 6-5. *Error message displayed during initialization*

Utility Composables

Following the same principle as the useCounter() composable (and its derived composables), let's write other composables that will serve as utility composables, as they can be used in various applications. These include the following:

1. useFetch(): Performs an HTTP request.

2. useWindowSize(): Determines the size of the window.

3. useGeolocation(): Determines the current geolocation.

Let's start with the first proposed composable, which is useFetch().

useFetch( ) Composable for Performing an HTTP Request

The useFetch(url) composable allows for making an HTTP request to a specified URL (url parameter) using the fetch(url) method defined in JavaScript. The composable returns a startFetch() method that initiates the HTTP request, and the asynchronous result will be returned by the startFetch() method.

Let's create the MyCountries component that utilizes the useFetch() composable to retrieve results. We will use the URL https://restcountries.com/v3.1/all, which was employed in Chapter 4 to fetch the list of countries worldwide.

MyCountries component using the useFetch() composable (file src/components/MyCountries.vue)

```
<script setup>
import useFetch from "../composables/useFetch"

import { ref } from "vue";
const data = ref();

const url = "https://restcountries.com/v3.1/all";
const [startFetch] = useFetch(url);

const initData = async () => {
  data.value = await startFetch();
}

</script>
```

```
<template>

<button @click="initData">Start Fetch</button>
<br><br>
<b>Data</b> : {{data}}

</template>
```

The MyCountries component utilizes the useFetch() composable, hence the import statement import useFetch.

The useFetch() composable returns the startFetch() method, allowing the initiation of data retrieval from the server using the URL provided in useFetch(url).

The "Start Fetch" button on the page triggers the data retrieval, which will be displayed in the reactive variable data. To achieve this, the initData() method is created, called upon clicking the button. This method invokes the startFetch() method obtained from the composable, and the startFetch() method returns the data read from the server. To manage the asynchronous nature of exchanges between the client and the server, the async and await keywords of JavaScript are utilized within this method.

Let us now write the useFetch() composable used in the MyCountries component. As indicated previously, it should return an asynchronous startFetch() function that retrieves data from the server in JSON format.

useFetch() composable (file src/composables/useFetch.js)

```
const useFetch = (url) => {
  const startFetch = async () => {
    const res = await fetch(url);
    const d = await res.text();
    return JSON.parse(d);  // Returning the data read from the
    server in JSON format
  }
```

```
  return [startFetch];
}
```

```
export default useFetch;
```

The App component is, of course, modified to integrate the MyCountries component:

App component (file src/App.vue)

```
<script setup>

import MyCountries from './components/MyCountries.vue'

</script>

<template>

<MyCountries />

</template>
```

Let's run the program. The MyCountries component will be displayed with the "Start Fetch" button:

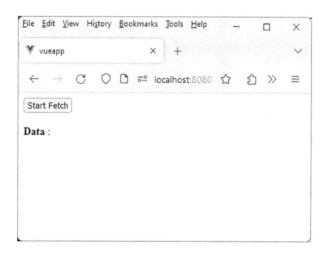

Figure 6-6. *MyCountries component*

Clicking on the "Start Fetch" button retrieves the list of countries from the server and displays it as a table in the reactive `data` variable.

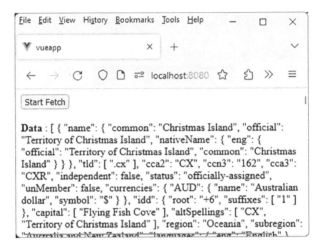

Figure 6-7. *List of retrieved countries displayed by the useFetch()* *composable*

useFetchCountries( ) Composable Derived from useFetch( )

The previous useFetch() composable serves as a starting point to create another composable specifically designed to display only the country names, which are located in the name.common properties of each array element.

The new composable is named useFetchCountries(url). It utilizes the previous url parameter and returns a fetchCountries() function that retrieves an array containing the names of the countries, sorted alphabetically.

The MyCountries component is modified to accommodate the newly used composable:

MyCountries component (file src/components/MyCountries.vue)

```
<script setup>
import useFetchCountries from "../composables/
useFetchCountries"

import { ref } from "vue";
const data = ref();

const url = "https://restcountries.com/v3.1/all";
const [startFetch] = useFetchCountries(url);

const initData = async () => {
  data.value = await startFetch();
}

</script>

<template>

<button @click="initData">Start Fetch</button>
<br><br>
<b>Data</b> : {{data}}

</template>
```

Note that the name of the function returned by the composable can remain the same as before, as only the position in the returned array is relevant, as we have previously explained.

The new useFetchCountries(url) composable is written as follows:

**useFetchCountries composable (file src/composables/
useFetchCountries.js)**

```
import useFetch from "./useFetch";

const useFetchCountries = (url) => {
  const [startFetch] = useFetch(url);
  let countries;
```

```
const startFetchCountries = async () => {
  const data = await startFetch();
  countries = data.map(function(elem) {
    return elem.name.common;   // Retain only the common.name
    property
  });
  // In ascending alphabetical order
  countries = countries.sort((n1, n2) => {
    if (n1 > n2) return 1;
    if (n1 < n2) return -1;
    return 0;
  });
  return countries;
}
return [startFetchCountries];
}

export default useFetchCountries;
```

The useFetchCountries() composable utilizes the useFetch()
composable. The new function startFetchCountries() provided by the
composable returns an array of all country names, ordered in ascending
alphabetical order.

Let's see if it works after clicking the "Start Fetch" button:

Figure 6-8. *List of retrieved country names displayed as an array*

Now that the useFetchCountries() composable provides a function that returns country names as a JavaScript array, we can modify the MyCountries component to display the list of countries as an HTML list. The v-for directive in Vue.js will allow us to achieve this.

The MyCountries component is thus modified:

Display countries as an HTML list (file src/components/MyCountries.vue)

```
<script setup>
import useFetchCountries from "../composables/
useFetchCountries"

import { ref } from "vue";
const data = ref();

const url = "https://restcountries.com/v3.1/all";
const [startFetch] = useFetchCountries(url);

const initData = async () => {
  data.value = await startFetch();
}
```

```
</script>

<template>

<button @click="initData">Start Fetch</button>
<br><br>
<b>Data</b> :
<ul>
<li v-for="(country, i) in data" :key="i">{{country}}</li>
</ul>

</template>
```

The list of countries is now displayed in HTML format:

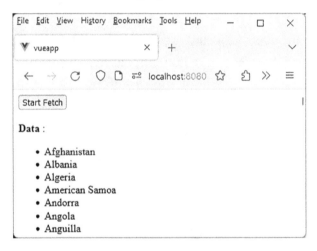

Figure 6-9. *List of countries displayed in HTML format*

useWindowSize( ) Composable for Real-Time Window Size Information

The useWindowSize() composable returns a reactive variable, windowSize, represented by an object { width, height }, indicating the width and height of the window in which the application is running, respectively.

If the window is resized, the reactive variable windowSize updates in real time.

The useWindowSize() composable is created in the src/composables directory.

**useWindowSize() composable (file src/composables/
useWindowSize.js)**

```
import { ref, onMounted, onBeforeUnmount } from "vue";

const useWindowSize = () => {
  const windowSize = ref({
    width: window.innerWidth,
    height: window.innerHeight,
  });

  const updateWindowSize = () => {
    windowSize.value = {
      width: window.innerWidth,
      height: window.innerHeight,
    };
  };

  onMounted(() => {
    window.addEventListener('resize', updateWindowSize);
  });

  onBeforeUnmount(() => {
    window.removeEventListener('resize', updateWindowSize);
  });

  return windowSize;
}

export default useWindowSize;
```

The useWindowSize() composable returns the reactive variable windowSize. It is not placed in an array since it is the sole value returned by the composable.

The composable is utilized in the MyCounter component.

Usage of the useWindowSize() composable (file src/components/ MyCounter.vue)

```
<script setup>

import useWindowSize from '../composables/useWindowSize';

const windowSize = useWindowSize();

</script>

<template>

<h3>MyCounter Component</h3>

Window size: <b>{{windowSize}}</b>

</template>
```

The App component displays the MyCounter component:

App component (file src/App.vue)

```
<script setup>

import MyCounter from './components/MyCounter.vue'

</script>

<template>

<MyCounter />

</template>
```

As the window is resized, the new dimensions are displayed in real time within the window:

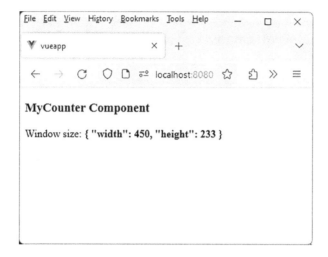

Figure 6-10. *Usage of the useWindowSize() composable*

The useWindowSize() composable serves as a starting point to crea format and determining whether to display the application on a mobile phone or a conventional website.

useGeolocation( ) Composable for Obtaining User Latitude and Longitude

The useGeolocation() composable will be valuable for determining the geographical location of the user.

useGeolocation() composable (file src/composables/ useGeolocation.js)

```
import { ref, onMounted } from "vue";
```

```
const useGeolocation = () => {
  const latitude = ref(null);
  const longitude = ref(null);

  const handleGeolocation = (position) => {
    latitude.value = position.coords.latitude;
    longitude.value = position.coords.longitude;
  };

  const errorGeolocation = (error) => {
    console.log("Geolocation error:", error.message);
  };

  onMounted(() => {
    if (navigator.geolocation) {
      navigator.geolocation.getCurrentPosition(handleGeolocati
      on, errorGeolocation);
    } else {
      console.log("Geolocation is not available in this
      browser.");
    }
  });

  return [latitude, longitude];
}

export default useGeolocation;
```

We define two reactive variables, latitude and longitude, which will be returned by the composable. The browser's geolocation API is utilized to retrieve the user's GPS coordinates.

To initiate geolocation upon program startup, we use the onMounted() method of the composable, where the processing is performed.

The MyCounter component, which uses the composable and displays the returned data, is as follows:

Usage of the useGeolocation() composable (file src/components/MyCounter.vue)

```
<script setup>
import useGeolocation from '../composables/useGeolocation';
const [latitude, longitude] = useGeolocation();
</script>

<template>

<h3>MyCounter Component</h3>

Latitude: <b>{{latitude}}</b>
<br>
Longitude: <b>{{longitude}}</b>
<br>

</template>
```

Let's run the program. After granting the browser access to geolocation, we obtain the following:

Figure 6-11. *Usage of the useGeolocation() composable*

The latitude and longitude have been updated in the component.

useGeolocationWithDetails( ) Composable Derived from useGeolocation( )

Let's enhance the previous useGeolocation() composable by providing not only the latitude and longitude but also the corresponding country and city. For this purpose, we create the new composable useGeolocationWithDetails().

To achieve this, we use a new API from the site https://nominatim. openstreetmap.org/reverse. By specifying latitude and longitude in the URL, it returns a JSON object containing, among other things, the corresponding country and city.

For example, using the following URL in a browser: https:// nominatim.openstreetmap.org/reverse?format=json&lat=30.267153&l on=-97.7430608.

Figure 6-12. *Usage of the API* `https://nominatim.openstreetmap.org/reverse`

The previous location indicates that we are located in the United States, in the city of Austin, Texas.

To implement this new composable, we will use the previous `useGeolocation()` composable, which provides the current latitude and longitude. Then, by passing these two values to the URL `https://nominatim.openstreetmap.org/reverse`, we receive in return the country, city, etc., corresponding to the indicated GPS coordinates.

The MyCounter component is modified to use the new composable useGeolocationWithDetails() and display the country and city.

Display the country and city (file src/components/MyCounter.vue)

```
<script setup>

import useGeolocationWithDetails from '../composables/
useGeolocationWithDetails';

const [latitude, longitude, country, city] =
useGeolocationWithDetails();

</script>

<template>

<h3>MyCounter Component</h3>

Latitude : <b>{{latitude}}</b>
<br>
Longitude : <b>{{longitude}}</b>
<br>
Country : <b>{{country}}</b>
<br>
City : <b>{{city}}</b>
<br>

</template>
```

The new useGeolocationWithDetails() composable returns an array [latitude, longitude, country, city]. Each value in the array corresponds to a reactive variable displayed in the component.

Let's now write the useGeolocationWithDetails() composable. It utilizes the previous useGeolocation() composable to obtain the latitude and longitude to be used in determining the corresponding country and city.

296

**useGeolocationWithDetails() composable (file src/composables/
useGeolocationWithDetails.js)**

```
import { ref, watchEffect } from "vue";

import useGeolocation from '../composables/useGeolocation';

const useGeolocationWithDetails = () => {
  const [latitude, longitude] = useGeolocation();
  const country = ref("");
  const city = ref("");

  // To find the country and city corresponding to the
latitude/longitude
  watchEffect(async ()=>{
    if (latitude.value && longitude.value) {
      const response = await fetch(
        `https://nominatim.openstreetmap.org/reverse?format=jso
        n&lat=${latitude.value}&lon=${longitude.value}`
      );
      const data = await response.json();
      if (data && data.address && data.address.country) {
        country.value = data.address.country;
      }
      if (data && data.address) {
        city.value = data.address.city || data.address.town;
      }
    }
  });

  return [latitude, longitude, country, city];
}

export default useGeolocationWithDetails;
```

The interesting part of this composable lies in using the watchEffect() method. When you write the statement const [latitude, longitude] = useGeolocation();, it doesn't mean that the variables latitude and longitude are immediately initialized. We need to wait for geolocation to be performed in the useGeolocation() composable.

How do we know when these variables, latitude and longitude, have been initialized? Since they are reactive, we can observe their value changes using the watchEffect(callback) method. The callback function provided as a parameter is called on the initial invocation of watchEffect(). This allows Vue.js to determine the reactive variables used in the callback, which will be the ones observed.

Using the statement if (latitude.value && longitude.value) within watchEffect() indicates that we are observing the reactive variables latitude and longitude. The subsequent processing is straightforward. When these variables change, we retrieve the country name from the address.country field, and similarly, we could retrieve the city from the address.city or address.town fields.

The result is as follows:

Figure 6-13. *Usage of the useGeolocationWithDetails() composable*

The country and city names are also displayed in the component.

useMap( ) Composable for Displaying the GPS Location Map

Creating the useGeolocationWithDetails() composable gives us the idea to create a new composable for displaying the map of the location indicated by GPS coordinates. Let's name this new composable useMap().

To display the map, we can use various APIs. Among them, we have chosen Leaflet because it does not require an API key to function.

Step 1: Install the Leaflet API

To use Leaflet, simply install it with the npm install leaflet command. This command is executed from the directory of the Vue.js application (in this case, the vueapp directory).

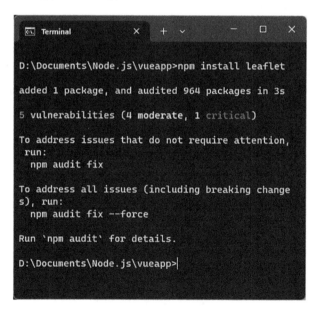

Figure 6-14. Installing the Leaflet API in the Vue.js application

Step 2: Using the Leaflet API

Leaflet uses a JavaScript API and CSS style files to function.

1. To use the JavaScript API, import Leaflet into our program using the statement `import L from "leaflet"`. The methods of the Leaflet API are accessible through the `L` object.

2. To use Leaflet's CSS files, import them into the main `index.html` file of the application. The `index.html` file using Leaflet's CSS files becomes as follows:

Using Leaflet styles in the Vue.js application (file src/public/index.html)

```
<!DOCTYPE html>
<html lang="">
  <head>
    <meta charset="utf-8">
    <meta http-equiv="X-UA-Compatible" content="IE=edge">
    <meta name="viewport" content="width=device-width,initial-scale=1.0">
    <link rel="icon" href="<%= BASE_URL %>favicon.ico">

    <!-- To include the Leaflet CSS -->
    <link rel="stylesheet" href="https://unpkg.com/leaflet@1.7.1/dist/leaflet.css" />

    <title><%= htmlWebpackPlugin.options.title %></title>
  </head>
  <body>
    <noscript>
```

```
  <strong>We're sorry but <%= htmlWebpackPlugin.options.
  title %> doesn't work properly without JavaScript
  enabled. Please enable it to continue.</strong>
 </noscript>

 <div id="app"></div>
 <!-- built files will be auto injected -->
</body>
</html>
```

To include Leaflet's CSS styles, you can use the `<link>` tag in the application.

Now, let's explore how to use Leaflet in the `useMap()` composable.

Step 3: Writing the useMap( ) Composable

To display a map, Leaflet requires the following:

1. The latitude and longitude of the location to be displayed

2. The ID of the DOM element in which to display the map

3. The desired zoom level to display the map

The `useMap(latitude, longitude, idMap)` composable displays the desired map in the DOM element with the specified `idMap`. By default, we will use a zoom level of 13.

In return, the composable provides the `map` object created by Leaflet. This object allows, for example, the use of the statement `map.remove()` to remove any previously displayed map in the specified DOM element.

The `useMap()` composable can be written as follows:

301

useMap composable (file src/composables/useMap.js)

```
import L from "leaflet"

const useMap = (latitude, longitude, idMap) => {
  const zoom = 13;

  // To position the map at the indicated location
  const map = L.map(idMap).setView([latitude,
  longitude], zoom);

  // To display the corresponding map
  L.tileLayer("https://a.tile.openstreetmap.org/{z}/{x}/
  {y}.png", {
    maxZoom: 20,
  }).addTo(map);

  // To display a marker on the map to indicate the specified
  location
  L.marker([latitude, longitude]).addTo(map);

  // We return the map object created by Leaflet
  return map;
}

export default useMap;
```

We modify the MyCounter component to use the useMap() composable:

Using the useMap() composable (file src/components/MyCounter.vue)

```
<script setup>

import useGeolocationWithDetails from "../composables/
useGeolocationWithDetails.js"
import useMap from "../composables/useMap.js"
```

```
import { onMounted, watchEffect } from "vue";

const [latitude, longitude, country, city] =
useGeolocationWithDetails();

// The onMounted() method ensures that the "map" DOM element is
correctly inserted into the DOM.
onMounted(()=>{
  // The watchEffect() method waits for the latitude and
  longitude to be properly initialized.
  watchEffect(()=>{
    if (latitude.value && longitude.value) useMap(latitude.
    value, longitude.value, "map");
  });
});

</script>

<template>

<h3>MyCounter Component</h3>

<p>Map around the city: <b v-show="city">{{city}} -
{{country}}</b></p>
<div id="map" />

</template>

<style scoped>
#map {
  height: 300px;
  width: 100%;
}
</style>
```

We are using the following two composables:

1. The `useGeolocationWithDetails()` composable retrieves the latitude, longitude, city, and country of the location where we are geolocated.

2. The `useMap()` composable displays the map of the location obtained by the previous composable.

Additionally, we are using the `onMounted()` and `watchEffect()` methods of Vue.js:

1. The `onMounted()` method ensures that the DOM element associated with the map (defined by `<div id="map" />`) is correctly inserted into the DOM, as Leaflet cannot begin to display the map if this element is not present.

2. The `watchEffect(callback)` method observes changes in the values of reactive variables used in the associated callback function. Since the `latitude` and `longitude` obtained by `useGeolocationWithDetails()` are not acquired sequentially, we observe the associated reactive variables.

Let's verify the functionality of the program:

Figure 6-15. *Usage of the useMap() composable to display the map of the location*

Now, let's see how to enhance the program by creating a v-map directive that internally uses the useMap() composable.

Step 4: v-map Directive Using the useMap() Composable

The previous program is functional. However, it requires writing instructions like the ones previously written in onMounted() or watchEffect(), which could be localized in a directive rather than within the component itself. This is the purpose of the new v-map directive.

You would use this directive in the MyCounter component as follows:

Using the v-map directive (file src/components/MyCounter.vue)

```
<script setup>

import useGeolocationWithDetails from "../composables/
useGeolocationWithDetails.js"

const [latitude, longitude, country, city] =
useGeolocationWithDetails();

</script>

<template>

<h3>MyCounter Component</h3>

<p>Map around the city: <b v-show="city">{{city}} -
{{country}}</b></p>
<div v-map="{latitude:latitude,longitude:longitude}"
id="map" />

</template>

<style scoped>
#map {
  height: 300px;
  width: 100%;
}
</style>
```

The previous `<div id="map" />` element is now written as

```
<div v-map="{latitude:latitude,longitude:longitude}"
id="map" />
```

This `<div>` element now uses the `v-map` directive, to which we pass the latitude and longitude returned by `useGeolocationWithDetails()` as its value. The `v-map` directive internally retrieves these values using the `binding` parameter through `binding.value.latitude` and `binding.value.longitude`.

It is worth noting that the component will be automatically refreshed when the `v-map` directive has its value changed, thanks to the reactive variables. Therefore, the map will be displayed with the final values of latitude and longitude when they are obtained by the `useGeolocationWithDetails()` composable.

The `v-map` directive utilizes the `useMap()` composable. It is written as follows:

v-map directive (file src/directives/map.js)

```
import useMap from "../composables/useMap.js"

const map = {
  updated(el, binding) {
    const latitude = binding.value.latitude;
    const longitude = binding.value.longitude;
    if (latitude && longitude) {
      if (el._map) el._map.remove();
      el._map = useMap(latitude, longitude, el.id);
    }
    else if (el._map) {
      el._map.remove();
      el._map = null;
    }
  }
}

export default map;
```

We use the updated() method of the directive's lifecycle. We check whether the latitude and longitude are known, and if so, we display the map using the useMap() composable. The map object returned by useMap() is stored as a property of the DOM element (in el._map) to clear a previous map that may have been displayed in this element (otherwise, Leaflet returns an error).

To make the directive usable, it needs to be inserted into the directives.js file, as explained in the previous chapter:

Adding the v-map directive (file src/directives.js)

```
import focus from "./directives/focus";
import integersOnly from "./directives/integers-only";
import maxValue from "./directives/max-value";
import clearable from "./directives/clearable";
import timer from "./directives/timer";
import map from "./directives/map";

export default {
  focus,
  integersOnly,
  maxValue,
  clearable,
  timer,
  map,
}
```

Let's verify the proper functioning of the entire system:

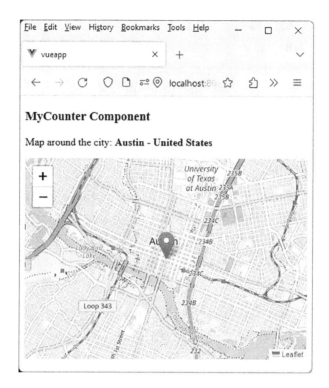

Figure 6-16. *Usage of the v-map directive*

Conclusion

In this chapter, we explored in detail the creation and usage of composables in Vue.js. We discussed why composables are valuable and how they differ from directives, being complementary. We then followed the steps to create and enhance Vue.js composables, illustrating this through concrete examples.

We also discovered utility composables that facilitate the management of common tasks such as HTTP requests, monitoring window size, geolocation, and displaying maps.

One of the most interesting examples was the creation of the `useMap()` composable to display maps based on GPS location using the Leaflet API. We followed a step-by-step process to create this composable, gaining insights into how to integrate third-party libraries into Vue.js.

Finally, we saw how to use the composables we created by incorporating them into custom directives, such as `v-map`, to make their usage even more user-friendly.

In conclusion, composables are a powerful way to abstract reusable logic and simplify the development of Vue.js applications. They provide an elegant way to handle complexity while keeping the code clean and modular. By mastering the creation and usage of composables, you can significantly enhance your productivity in Vue.js development. The ball is in your court!

CHAPTER 7

JavaScript Reminders

Before delving into the world of Vue.js, it is important to recall the fundamentals of JavaScript. This section is intended to assist you in refreshing your memory and getting up to speed on the key concepts of JavaScript that are utilized throughout the book.

We will cover essential concepts such as variables, arrays, objects, arrow functions, and modules. Additionally, we will explore more advanced concepts like asynchronous functions.

- If you are already familiar with JavaScript, this section will help you recall and ensure that you have the necessary basics to understand Vue.js code examples.

- If you are new to the world of JavaScript, this section will provide you with a solid foundation to comprehend the concepts used throughout the book.

Ready to reinforce your JavaScript knowledge? Let's begin!

Using the Keywords let and var in JavaScript

In JavaScript, `let` and `var` are two keywords used to declare variables. The main difference between them lies in the variable's scope.

© Eric Sarrion 2024
E. Sarrion, *Master Vue.js in 6 Days*, https://doi.org/10.1007/979-8-8688-0364-2_7

The `var` keyword has a function scope, meaning that the variable is accessible inside the function where it is declared, as well as anywhere inside that function.

For example:

Using var to define a variable

```
function example() {
  var x = 10;
  if (true) {
    var x = 20; // The variable x is accessible inside the
                function example()
  }
  console.log(x); // Displays 20
}
```

In this example, the variable x is declared inside the function example(), but it is also accessible within the if block, because var has function scope. Therefore, writing var x = 20; does not create a new variable, as the variable x was declared earlier and is directly accessible within the if block. By writing var x = 20;, we are only modifying the value of the previously created variable.

On the other hand, the `let` keyword has block scope, which means the variable is accessible only within the block in which it is declared and in all nested blocks inside that block.

For example:

Using let to define a variable

```
function example() {
  let x = 10;
  if (true) {
    let x = 20; // The variable x is accessible only within the
                "if" block
```

```
    }
    console.log(x); // Displays 10
}
```

In this example, the variable x is declared inside the function example(). However, the second declaration of x inside the if block creates a new variable x, which is accessible only within that block. The variable x outside the if block retains its initial value of 10.

In summary, the main difference between let and var is the variable's scope: var has function scope, and let has block scope. It is generally recommended to use let rather than var in JavaScript code, as it provides better control over variable scope and helps avoid accidental variable reuse across different blocks.

Using the const Keyword in JavaScript

In JavaScript, the const keyword is used to declare a variable that cannot be reassigned after its initial value has been assigned. It creates a variable with a constant, unchangeable reference to a value. This means that once a value is assigned to a const variable, you cannot reassign it to a different value later in the code.

Here's an explanation of how the const keyword works and its key characteristics.

When declaring a variable using const, you must immediately assign a value to it. Unlike the var or let keywords, you cannot declare a const variable without initializing it.

Declaration and Initialization

```
const pi = 3.14159;
```

Once a value is assigned to a const variable, its value cannot be changed. Attempting to reassign a const variable will result in an error.

Value Immutability

```
const pi = 3.14159;
pi = 3.14; // This will result in an error
```

Like variables declared with `let`, `const` variables are block-scoped. They are only accessible within the block (enclosed by curly braces) where they are defined.

Block Scope

```
if (true) {
  const message = "Hello";
  console.log(message); // OK
}
console.log(message); // Error: 'message' is not defined
```

You cannot declare another variable with the same name in the same scope if you've already declared it with `const`.

No Redeclaration

```
const value = 42;
const value = 100; // Error: Identifier 'value' has already
                   been declared
```

When using `const` with objects and arrays, the reference to the object or array itself is immutable, but the properties or elements within the object or array can still be modified.

Modifying object's properties and array's elements

```
const person = { name: "Alice", age: 30 };
person.age = 31; // Valid, modifies a property inside
the object
const numbers = [1, 2, 3];
numbers.push(4); // Valid, adds an element to the array
```

In summary, the `const` keyword is used to declare variables that are meant to remain constant after their initial assignment. It ensures immutability of the variable reference, but the properties or elements within objects and arrays declared with `const` can still be modified. Use `const` for values that should not be changed throughout the scope of the variable.

Manipulating Objects in JavaScript

In JavaScript, structuring and destructuring objects are techniques that allow for efficient data manipulation.

Step 1: Structuring an Object

Structuring an object involves defining a data structure for that object. You can create an object with a list of properties and their corresponding values. For example, you can create a `person` object with properties like name, age, and `city` as follows:

Creating the person object

```
const person = {
  name: "Gaby",
  age: 40,
  city: "Austin"
};
```

This allows us to access the values `person.name` (which is "Gaby"), `person.age` (which is 40), and `person.city` (which is "Austin").

Step 2: Object Destructuring

Object destructuring, on the other hand, allows you to extract object properties and use them independently. For instance, you can extract the name and age properties from the person object as follows:

Destructuring the person object

```
const { name, age } = person;
```

In this example, we create two variables, name and age, that correspond to properties of the same names in the person object. We can now use these variables independently of the rest of the object.

Destructuring can also be used to pass arguments to a function in a more concise way. For example, you can create a function that takes an object person as an argument and displays the person's name and age:

Using destructuring in function definition

```
function displayNameAge({ name, age }) {
  console.log(`The name is ${name} and the age is ${age}`);
}
```

In this example, we use destructuring to extract the properties name and age from the person object that is passed as an argument. We can now call this function with the person object as follows:

Using the function

```
displayNameAge(person);
```

This will display "The name is Gaby and the age is 40" in the console.

In summary, object structuring and destructuring in JavaScript are powerful techniques that allow for efficient and concise data manipulation.

Step 3: Passing Objects As Function Parameters

In JavaScript, the notation { key1, key2 } is used in function parameters to perform object destructuring. This notation allows you to destructure a literal object by extracting the values associated with the specified properties and assigning them to variables with the same names as the properties.

Here's an example to illustrate its usage:

Object as a function parameter

```
function displayDetails({ name, age }) {
  console.log(`Name: ${name}`);
  console.log(`Age: ${age}`);
}

const person = {
  name: "Gaby",
  age: 40,
  city: "Austin",
  profession: "Developer",
};

displayDetails(person);    // Displays "Name: Gaby" and
                           "Age: 40"
```

In this example, the displayDetails() function takes an object as a parameter and destructures the object to extract values associated with the name and age properties. The extracted values are then used to display the person's details.

It's important to note that if a specified property in the destructuring notation does not exist in the object, its value will be undefined. Additionally, it's possible to rename the extracted variables using the syntax { property: newVariable }.

317

In summary, the { key1, key2 } notation in function parameters allows for object destructuring, extracting values associated with specified properties. This leads to more concise and readable code, avoiding direct property access within the function body.

Step 4: Using the "..." Notation with Objects

Let's now explain the "..." (three consecutive dots) notation with objects. The "..." notation in JavaScript, also known as the spread or rest operator, is used to spread or gather the elements of an array or an object.

When used with an object, the "..." notation creates a shallow copy of the original object, including all its properties and their values. For example:

Using the "..." notation with objects

```
const object1 = { x: 1, y: 2 };
const object2 = { ...object1 };
console.log(object2);      // { x: 1, y: 2 }
```

In this example, the "..." notation is used to spread the properties of object1 into object2. This creates a shallow copy of object1, with the same properties and values.

If you write const object2 = object1;, it does not do the same thing at all! This statement creates a variable object2 that has the same memory reference as object1, thus referencing the same content as object1. If you modify the content of object1 or object2, the other object will be modified in the same way.

The "..." notation can also be used to merge multiple objects into one. For example:

Merging objects with "..."

```
const object1 = { x: 1, y: 2 };
const object2 = { z: 3 };
```

```
const object3 = { ...object1, ...object2 };
console.log(object3);    // { x: 1, y: 2, z: 3 }
```

In this example, the "..." notation is used to merge the properties of objects object1 and object2 into a new object object3.

It's important to note that the "..." notation creates only a shallow copy of the original object. If the object contains properties that are themselves objects or arrays, these properties are not deeply copied and are still shared between the original object and the copy (since it's the references to objects or arrays that are copied, thus shared between the original object and the new object).

Manipulating Arrays in JavaScript

In JavaScript, an array is a data structure that allows you to store and access multiple elements as an ordered list.

Step 1: Structuring an Array

Structuring arrays in JavaScript refers to creating, initializing, and manipulating arrays to store and organize data.

Creating an array in JavaScript can be done in several ways. The most common way is to declare an empty array [ ] and add elements using the push() method. For example:

Creating an array using the push() method

```
let array = [];
array.push(1);
array.push(2);
array.push(3);
console.log(array);    // [1, 2, 3]
```

Another common method to create an array is by using the array literal notation, which allows you to declare and initialize an array in a single step. For example:

Creating an array using []

```
let array = [1, 2, 3];
console.log(array);    // [1, 2, 3]
```

Step 2: Array Destructuring

Array destructuring in JavaScript refers to extracting elements from an array into separate variables. This feature is useful for manipulating arrays in a more concise and readable manner. For example:

Array destructuring into separate variables

```
let array = [1, 2, 3];
let [firstElement, secondElement, thirdElement] = array;
console.log(firstElement);    // 1
console.log(secondElement);   // 2
console.log(thirdElement);    // 3
```

Step 3: Using the "..." Notation with Arrays

Destructuring also allows you to retrieve a portion of an array using the "..." syntax. For example:

Destructuring an array using the "..." notation

```
let array = [1, 2, 3, 4, 5];
let [a, b, ...rest] = array;
console.log(a);      // 1
console.log(b);      // 2
console.log(rest);   // [3, 4, 5]
```

In this example, the "..." notation is used to retrieve the remaining elements of the array after assigning the first two elements to the variables a and b. The variable rest will contain the elements 3, 4, and 5 as an array, that is, [3, 4, 5].

Using Import and Export of Modules in JavaScript

In JavaScript, modules are code files that can contain functions, variables, and classes, which can be imported and used in other code files. Modules allow for structuring and organizing JavaScript code, making it more modular and easier to maintain.

There are several ways to define and import modules in JavaScript, but the most common method is using the import and export syntax. Modules can be exported using the export and export default keywords, and they can be imported using the import keyword.

Here's a simple example to illustrate the creation and usage of modules in JavaScript:

In the file myModule.js:

File: myModule.js

```
export const myVariable = "Hello world";

export function myFunction() {
  console.log("This is my function");
}

export default class MyClass {
  constructor() {
    console.log("This is my class");
  }
}
```

We export the variable myVariable, the function myFunction(), and the JavaScript class MyClass in the module myModule.js.

In another JavaScript file (e.g., test.js), we import these previously exported elements:

File: test.js

```
import { myVariable, myFunction } from './myModule.js';
import MyClass from './myModule.js';

console.log(myVariable);
myFunction();
const myInstance = new MyClass();
```

You can also write the import statement on a single line as follows:

File: test.js

```
import MyClass, { myVariable, myFunction } from './myModule.js';

console.log(myVariable);
myFunction();
const myInstance = new MyClass();
```

This way, we have access to the exported elements from the myModule.js file in the test.js file.

Step 1: Using Modules in HTML Files

To use JavaScript modules in an HTML file, we use the <script> tag with the type attribute set to "module".

Here's an example of HTML code that imports a module named myModule.js:

File: index.html

```
<!DOCTYPE html>
<html>
<head>
  <title>Example of Using Modules in HTML</title>
</head>
<body>

  <h1>Example of Using Modules in HTML</h1>

  <script type="module">
    import { myFunction } from './myModule.js';
    myFunction();
  </script>

</body>
</html>
```

The message "This is my function" is displayed in the browser console, demonstrating that the myFunction() is successfully accessible in the JavaScript code of the HTML file.

Step 2: Using the import Statement

The import statement is used in JavaScript to import modules from one JavaScript file to another. The basic syntax for importing a module is as follows:

Importing data from a module

```
import { variableName, functionName } from './path/to/module';
```

This syntax allows you to import specific variables or functions from a module. The path to the module should be relative to the current JavaScript file.

Here are some examples of using the `import` statement in JavaScript:

Using import in a module

```
// Importing a specific variable
import { myVariable } from './myModule.js';

console.log(myVariable);

// Importing multiple variables and a function
import { myVar1, myVar2, myFunction } from './myModule.js';

console.log(myVar1);
console.log(myVar2);
myFunction();

// Importing all exported variables and functions
import * as myModule from './myModule.js';

console.log(myModule.myVar1);
console.log(myModule.myVar2);
myModule.myFunction();
```

In these examples, the `import` statement is used to import specific variables and functions from a module. In the last example, all exported variables and functions are imported using the * operator, and an alias `myModule` is created to access the exported elements.

It's important to note that the `import` statement can only be used in a module context. A JavaScript file must be explicitly marked as a module by using the `type="module"` directive in the `<script>` tag of the calling HTML file.

Step 3: Using the export Statement

The export statement in JavaScript is used to export variables, functions, classes, or other elements from one JavaScript file to another. The exported elements can be used in other files by importing the module that contains them.

There are two main ways to export elements in JavaScript: using the export syntax or export default syntax.

The export syntax is used to export named elements. For example, to export a named variable myVariable and a named function myFunction from a file myModule.js, you can use the following syntax:

Exporting variables (file myModule.js)

```
export const myVariable = "Hello world";

export function myFunction() {
  console.log("This is my function");
}
```

The exported elements can then be imported into another file using the import statement. Here's an example:

Importing variables in another module

```
import { myVariable, myFunction } from './myModule.js';

console.log(myVariable); // Displays "Hello world"
myFunction(); // Displays "This is my function"
```

Step 4: Using the export default Statement

The export default syntax is used to export a default element from a module. For example, to export a default class from a file myModule.js, you can use the following syntax:

Using export default (file myModule.js)

```
export default class MyClass {
  constructor() {
    console.log("This is my class");
  }
}
```

In this example, the `MyClass` class is exported as the default. It can be imported into another file using the following syntax:

Importing variables in another module

```
import MyClass from './myModule.js';

const myInstance = new MyClass(); // Creates a new instance of
                                  the MyClass class
```

In summary, the `export` statement in JavaScript allows you to export elements from a module to make them available in other JavaScript files. It can be used to export variables, functions, classes, or other elements and can be combined with the `import` statement to create modular and reusable JavaScript applications.

Step 5: Difference Between export and export default Statements

The decision to use `export` or `export default` in JavaScript depends on how you want to expose module elements and import them later.

The `export` syntax is used to export multiple named elements from a module. This means that when a module is imported, the exported elements must be imported with their original names and enclosed in curly braces.

For example:

Using export then import

```
// In the file "myModule.js"
export const myVar1 = "Hello";
export const myVar2 = "World";
export function myFunction() {
```

```
  console.log("This is my function");
}

// In the file that imports the module
import { myVar1, myVar2, myFunction } from './myModule.js';
// with curly braces
```

In this example, the exported elements must be imported using their original names and enclosed in curly braces. If we try to import an element with a different name than the one specified in the export, an error will be generated.

The export default syntax is used to export a default element from a module. This means that the element exported as default can be imported later using a name of our choice. Only one element can be exported as default in a module, to avoid confusion.

JavaScript will understand that we want to import the default exported element in a module because we import it without using the curly braces notation, unlike elements exported using the export statement, which are imported with the curly braces notation.

For example:

Using export default then import

```
// In the file "myModule.js"
export default class MyClass {
  constructor() {
    console.log("This is my class");
  }
}

// In the file that imports the module
import MyCustomName from './myModule.js';    // without using
                                             curly braces

const myInstance = new MyCustomName();
```

In this example, the default exported element (the MyClass class) can be imported using a name of our choice (MyCustomName in this case). This can be useful if we want to give a more meaningful name to the imported element or avoid naming conflicts.

In summary, export is used to export multiple named elements from a module, while export default is used to export an element that will be considered the default one during import. The decision to use one or the other depends on how we want to expose module elements and how we want to import them into other files.

Using Arrow Functions in JavaScript

Arrow functions are a new function syntax introduced in ECMAScript 6 (ES6) to write functions in a more concise and readable way. Here are the main differences between arrow functions and traditional functions:

- **More Concise Syntax:** Arrow functions have a more concise syntax than traditional functions. Instead of the classic function() {function body}, arrow functions are written like this: () => {function body}.

- **No Bound this Keyword:** In traditional functions, the this keyword is bound to the object that calls the function. In arrow functions, this is bound to the lexical context in which the function is defined. This means that this in an arrow function refers to this in the parent scope (the value of this in an arrow function will be the same as that of the parent).

Apart from the concise writing aspect of arrow functions, the deciding factor to use them in JavaScript code is mostly the desired value for the this variable.

Let's now look at the syntax of these functions and then explain the value of this in each use case.

328

Step 1: Using Arrow Function Syntax

Let's start by examining the writing syntax of these functions. Here's an example:

Using traditional functions and arrow functions

```
// Traditional function to calculate the square of a number
function square(x) {
  return x * x;
}

// Arrow function to calculate the square of a number
const square2 = (x) => x * x;

// Using the function
console.log(square2(5)); // Result: 25
```

In this example, the first function is a traditional function that calculates the square of a number. The second function is the arrow version of the same function, which uses a more concise syntax. Both functions have the same functionality, but the arrow version is more concise and easier to read.

Note that the arrow function syntax includes parentheses around the parameters (in this case, x), followed by the arrow => and then the function body (in this case, x * x). The arrow version doesn't require the return keyword here because it automatically returns the calculated value.

Here's an example of an arrow function in JavaScript that uses the return statement:

Functions using the return keyword

```
// Traditional function to find the largest number in an array
function findLargest(array) {
  let largest = 0;
  for (let i = 0; i < array.length; i++) {
```

```
    if (array[i] > largest) {
      largest = array[i];
    }
  }
  return largest;
}

// Arrow function to find the largest number in an array
const findLargest2 = (array) => {
  let largest = 0;
  for (let i = 0; i < array.length; i++) {
    if (array[i] > largest) {
      largest = array[i];
    }
  }
  return largest;
}

// Using the function
console.log(findLargest2([4, 8, 2, 10, 5])); // Result: 10
```

In this example, the first function is a traditional function that finds the largest number in an array. The second function is the arrow version of the same function, which uses a more concise syntax. Both functions have the same functionality, and the arrow version also uses the return statement to return the calculated value.

Note that the arrow function syntax still includes parentheses around the parameters and the => arrow, but this time there are also curly braces to delimit the function body. The return statement is used to return the calculated value.

Step 2: Understanding the Value of this in Arrow Functions

The value of this in an arrow function is determined by the lexical context in which the function is defined, unlike traditional functions where this is determined by how the function is called.

In an arrow function, this refers to the value of this in the parent scope. This means that if the arrow function is defined within an object, for example, this in the arrow function refers to the parent object, not the object that calls the function.

Here's an example to illustrate this concept:

Values of this in traditional functions and arrow functions

```
const obj = {
  name: "John",
  sayHello: function() {
    console.log(`Hello, my name is ${this.name}`);  // "John"
    (this refers to obj)
  },
  sayHelloArrow: () => {
    console.log(`Hello, my name is ${this.name}`);  //
    undefined (this refers to the parent of obj)
  }
}

obj.sayHello();       // Result: "Hello, my name is John"
obj.sayHelloArrow();  // Result: "Hello, my name is undefined"
```

In this example, the object obj contains two functions: sayHello() and sayHelloArrow(). sayHello() is a regular function that uses this to access the name property of the object, while sayHelloArrow() is an arrow function that also uses this to access the name property.

331

When the sayHello() function is called, this refers to the obj object, allowing access to the name property and displaying it in the console. However, when the sayHelloArrow() function is called, this refers to the lexical context in which the function was defined, which is the global context in this case. Therefore, this.name is undefined in the arrow function, and undefined is displayed in the console.

Depending on the value of this that we want to access, we will use either a regular function or an arrow function.

Using the map( ) and filter( ) Methods of the JavaScript Array Class

The map(callback) and filter(callback) methods are two commonly used high-level functions in JavaScript for manipulating arrays (or collections of objects). Here's an explanation of each method:

Step 1: Using the map( ) Method

The map(callback) method creates a new array by applying a given function, here named callback(), to each element of the original array. The map() method takes a callback() function as a parameter.

The callback(element, index, array) function is then applied to each element of the original array. This function can take up to three arguments:

1. element: The current element being processed

2. index (optional): The index of the current element being processed in the array

3. array (optional): The original array on which we are applying the function

The `map()` method then returns a new array with the results of applying the `callback()` function to each original element. The resulting array will have the same length as the original array.

Here's a simple example for better understanding:

Using the map() method

```
const array = [1, 2, 3, 4, 5];

const doubledArray = array.map(function(element) {
  return element * 2;
});

console.log(doubledArray); // [2, 4, 6, 8, 10]
```

Here, we created an array with numbers, and then we used the `map()` method to create a new array with the same numbers, but multiplied by 2.

The `map()` method returns a new array constructed from the elements of the original array. The resulting array will have the same number of elements as the original array.

To reduce the number of elements in the resulting array, we will use the `filter()` method, which allows us to select the elements to be included in the resulting array (but without modifying them). Let's now look at the `filter()` method.

Step 2: Using the filter( ) Method

The `filter(callback)` method also creates a new array, but it filters the elements of the original array that satisfy a specified condition. This method also takes a `callback()` function as an argument, which will be applied to each element of the original array. This `callback()` function must return a boolean value: `true` if the element should be retained in the resulting array returned by the filter() method, `false` otherwise.

The callback(element, index, array) filter function also takes up to three arguments:

1. element: The current element being processed

2. index (optional): The index of the current element being processed in the array

3. array (optional): The original array on which the function is being applied

The filter() method then returns a new array with all the elements of the original array that satisfy the specified condition.

Here's a simple example to better understand:

Using the filter() method

```
const array = [1, 2, 3, 4, 5];

const filteredArray = array.filter(function(element) {
  return element % 2 === 0;   // Returns true if the element
                              is even (element is kept),
                              otherwise false
});
```

```
console.log(filteredArray); // [2, 4]
```

Here, we've created an array with numbers, and then we used the filter() method to create a new array with only the even numbers.

Using Promise Objects in JavaScript

Promise objects in JavaScript are used for handling asynchronous tasks, which are tasks that don't complete immediately. A Promise object represents a value that may not be available immediately but will be resolved (i.e., become available) at some point in the future.

Step 1: Promise Object Definition

Promise objects are often created as return values from functions because they provide a clearer and more structured way of handling asynchronous tasks.

When an asynchronous task is executed, it doesn't immediately return a result, as it needs to perform an operation that may take time (such as an HTTP request or file reading). While waiting for this operation to complete, the code that follows continues to execute, potentially causing synchronization and blocking issues.

Promise objects are used to address this issue. They provide a clear and structured way to handle asynchronous tasks by returning an object that represents the promise of a future result. This object can be used to attach callback functions that will be called once the asynchronous task is completed and the result is available.

For example, a function that performs an HTTP request can return a Promise object representing the promise of the request's result. Callbacks can then be attached to this Promise object using the then() and catch() methods to handle successful results (with then()) or errors (with catch()) that may occur during the execution of the asynchronous task.

In summary, the Promise object is created as a return value from a function to handle asynchronous tasks in a structured manner by returning an object representing the promise of a future result and attaching callbacks to handle results or errors.

A Promise object can be in one of the following three states:

1. "pending": The initial state of the Promise object, indicating that the asynchronous task is currently being executed

2. "resolved": The state in which the Promise object is resolved with a value

3. "rejected": The state in which the Promise object is rejected with an error reason

335

The Promise object exposes two methods for handling the results of the asynchronous task:

1. **The then() Method**: Used to handle the result if the task is successfully resolved

2. **The catch() Method**: Used to handle errors that occur if the task is rejected

By using Promise objects, it's possible to perform asynchronous tasks in JavaScript more efficiently and in a way that's easier to read and maintain.

To understand the use of Promise objects, let's take an example where we don't use them and then the same example where we do.

Step 2: Without Using Promise Objects

Here's an example without using Promise objects.

Let's say we want to load images from a server and display them in our application. Without Promise objects, we would have to use callbacks to handle the asynchrony:

Without using Promise objects

```
function loadImage(url, callback) {
  const img = new Image();
  img.onload = function() {
    // no error
    callback(null, img);
  };
  img.onerror = function() {
    // error
    callback("Unable to load the image.", null);
  };
```

```
  img.src = url;  // image loading
}

loadImage("https://example.com/image.jpg",
function(error, img) {
  if (error) {
    console.error(error);
  } else {
    document.body.appendChild(img);
  }
});
```

This example uses the Image object to load an image from the server. The loadImage() function takes the image URL and a callback function as arguments. This callback will be invoked once the image has been loaded. After the image is loaded, further processing can take place within the callback function, allowing for handling of the asynchrony. The callback function has two arguments: a possible error and the loaded img (image) itself.

Step 3: Using Promise Objects

Now, here's the same example using Promise objects:

Using Promise objects

```
function loadImage(url) {
  return new Promise(function(resolve, reject) {
    const img = new Image();
    img.onload = function() {
      // no error
      resolve(img);
    };
```

```
    img.onerror = function() {
      // error
      reject("Unable to load the image.");
    };
    img.src = url;  // image loading
  });
}

loadImage("https://example.com/image.jpg")
  .then(function(img) {
    document.body.appendChild(img);
  })
  .catch(function(error) {
    console.error(error);
  });
```

Here, the loadImage() function returns a Promise object that is
resolved with the image if the image loading succeeds, or is rejected with
an error message if it fails. By using the then() method, we can handle
the image once it has been loaded, and with the catch() method, we can
handle errors that occur.

The use of Promise objects in this example makes the code more
readable and easier to understand and provides simplified error handling.

Using async and await Statements in JavaScript

The async and await statements are features of JavaScript that make
working with Promise objects even more readable and understandable for
handling asynchronous tasks.

By using `async` and `await` statements, code can be written synchronously (i.e., with sequentially following instructions) while still effectively managing asynchronous tasks. The `async` statement is used to mark a function as asynchronous, allowing the use of the `await` statement within that function.

The `await` statement is used to wait for the resolution of a `Promise` object before continuing the code execution. This avoids the use of callbacks and results in code that is easier to read and understand.

For example, here's a usage example of `Promise` objects to make an HTTP request. We will then see how to write the same code using `async` and `await` statements.

Using Promise objects to make an HTTP request

```
fetch("https://api.example.com/data")
  .then(response => response.json())
  .then(data => console.log(data))
  .catch(error => console.error(error));
```

The `fetch()` and `json()` methods in JavaScript each return a `Promise` object, enabling the use of the `then()` and `catch()` methods on these methods.

Now, here's how we can rewrite this code using `async` and `await` statements:

Using async and await statements to make an HTTP request

```
async function getData() {
  try {
    const response = await fetch("https://api.example.
    com/data");
    const data = await response.json();
    console.log(data);
  } catch (error) {
```

```
    console.error(error);
  }
}
```

```
getData();
```

Here, the getData() function is marked as async, which allows (within the getData() function) the use of the await statement to wait for the resolution of Promise objects returned by the fetch() function and the json() method. The use of async and await statements enables writing code that is more readable and easier to understand while efficiently managing asynchronous tasks.

In summary, the use of async and await statements provides an easier and more readable way to utilize Promise objects for handling asynchronous tasks. This helps avoid the use of callbacks and reduces code complexity.

Creating an Asynchronous Function That Utilizes JavaScript's await Statement

Let's now see how to create an asynchronous function that can use the await statement. For this purpose, the function using await should fall into one of the following two cases:

1. The function returns a Promise object. This is the case, for example, with the previous fetch() and json() methods.

2. The function is declared with the async keyword. In this case, the function's return is always considered as a Promise object (even if the function returns another value).

Let's examine these two cases now.

Step 1: Using await with a Function That Returns a Promise Object

For await to be used with a function, the function can return a Promise object or be declared with the async keyword.

Here's an example of a function that returns a Promise object:

Function returning a Promise object

```
function wait(ms) {
  return new Promise(resolve => setTimeout(resolve, ms));
}
```

The wait(ms) function takes a number of milliseconds as input and returns a Promise object that will resolve after the specified number of milliseconds. The function utilizes the setTimeout() function to trigger the resolution of the Promise object after a specified delay.

To use the wait(ms) function with the await statement, you simply need to call it within a function marked with async, like this:

Usage of await in an async function

```
async function myFunction() {
  console.log("Start");    // Display "Start"
  await wait(2000);        // Wait for 2 seconds
  console.log("End");      // Then display "End" (after 2
  seconds)
}

myFunction();
```

This myFunction() function uses the await statement to wait for the resolution of the Promise object returned by the wait() function. The function prints "Start" to the console, waits for two seconds using await wait(2000), and then prints "End" to the console.

In cases where the wait(ms) function wants to return a value, you can simply provide that value ("value") as a parameter in the resolve(value) function call.

The wait(ms) function becomes the following:

Function wait(ms) that returns a value

```
function wait(ms) {
  return new Promise(resolve => setTimeout(() =>
  resolve("Waiting for " + ms + " ms"), ms));
}
```

We can no longer simply indicate setTimeout(resolve, ms) as before, because now we need to explicitly call the resolve() function and pass the return value as a parameter. Hence, the new syntax is written as setTimeout(() => resolve(value), ms).

We use the value returned by the wait(ms) function as follows:

Using the value returned by the wait(ms) function

```
async function myFunction() {
  console.log("Start");            // Display "Start"
  const result = await wait(2000); // Wait for 2 seconds
  console.log(result);             // Display the result
                                   // returned by the wait()
                                   // function
  console.log("End");              // Then display "End"
}

myFunction();
```

342

Step 2: Using await with a Function Declared with async

This is the second way to use the await statement when calling a function. The function must have been declared using the async keyword during its definition.

A function declared with the async keyword is considered to return a Promise object. Therefore, it can be used when called with the then() and catch() methods or used with the await keyword.

Using the myFunction() function with "await"

```javascript
function wait(ms) {
  return new Promise(resolve => setTimeout(() =>
  resolve("Waiting for " + ms + " ms"), ms));
}

async function myFunction() {
  console.log("Start");              // Display "Start"
  const result = await wait(2000);   // Wait for 2 seconds
  console.log(result);               // Display the result
                                     // returned by the wait()
                                     // function
  console.log("End");                // Then display "End"
  return "myFunction(): Waiting for 2000ms";
}

async function myMainFunction() {
  const result = await myFunction();
  console.log("result =", result);
}

myMainFunction();
```

343

Since the myFunction() is declared with async, it can be used within a new function called myMainFunction() using the await keyword. The result returned by myFunction() will be used as the return value in myMainFunction(), asynchronously (after waiting for two seconds).

The same process can be written using promises and the then() and catch() methods:

Using promises instead of await

```
function wait(ms) {
  console.log("wait(" + ms + ")");
  return new Promise(resolve => setTimeout(() =>
resolve("Waiting for " + ms + " ms"), ms));
}

async function myFunction() {
  console.log("Start");                 // Display "Start"
  const result = await wait(2000);  // Wait for 2 seconds
  console.log(result);              // Display the result
                                    // returned by the wait()
                                    // function
  console.log("End");                   // Then display "End"
  return "myFunction(): Waiting for 2000ms";
}

myFunction().then((res) => { console.log(res) });
```

The then(res) method used on the promise myFunction() allows retrieving the result of the promise, which is the string "myFunction(): Waiting for 2000ms", in the parameter res.

Conclusion

In this chapter, we have covered the fundamentals of JavaScript, which are the ones used in programs written with Vue.js. This knowledge is necessary to harness the full power of Vue.js in our applications.

Index

A

addEventListener() method, 219

App component, 24, 29
  HelloWorld, 26, 34
  import statement, 35
  MyCounter component, 34, 42, 283, 290
  versions, 35

app.directive(name, callback) method, 210

Applications
  App component, 178, 181
  inject() method, 199, 200, 202
  filter list of countries, 187–189
  focus to input field, 202–204
  MyCountries component, 178–181
  provide() method, 199, 200, 202
  REST API, 173, 174
  retrieve list of countries, 182–186
  screens, list of countries, 174–177
  watchEffect() method, 194–199
  watch() method, 188–194

Arrays
  "..." notation, 320, 321
  destructuring, 320
  structuring, 319, 320

Arrow functions, 328
  syntax, 329, 330
  vs. traditional functions, 328
  value of this, 331, 332

Asynchronous function
  await statement
    async keyword, 343, 344
    Promise object, 341, 342
  cases, 340

B

Backgroundcolor
  argument, 243–245
Bold modifier, 227, 233–235

C

callback() function, 332, 333
catch() methods, 184, 336, 338
Components
  aforementioned methods, 52
  App component, 23, 34 (*see also* App component)
  Composition API syntax, 35
  computed properties, 48–50

© Eric Sarrion 2024
E. Sarrion, *Master Vue.js in 6 Days*, https://doi.org/10.1007/979-8-8688-0364-2

D

defineEmits()
    method, 166
defineProps()
    method, 88, 90, 94
defineProps(["count",
    "doubleCount"])
    method, 103
defineProps(["index"])
    method, 121
DevTools, 39
    console window, 40, 41
    extension, 40
    installation, Firefox, 39
Directives, 96, 264
    attributes
        end attribute, 86, 88–91
        init attribute, 85, 86, 88–91
        limits attribute, 91, 92, 94
        object as
            attributes, 92–95
    HTML element, 95
    v-bind (*see* v-bind directive)
    v-for (*see* v-for directive)
    v-if and v-else (*see* v-if and
        v-else directives)
    v-model (*see* v-model directive)
    v-show directive, 113
directives.js file, 214
Document Object Model (DOM),
        4–8, 23, 51, 55, 148, 182,
        202, 203, 208–211, 219, 277,
        279, 301, 304

E

elem.name.common, 183
Event-handling function, 151,
        153, 154
Event object
    in event-handling functions
        clear field content on click,
            158, 159
        filter pressed key, 154–156
        handle content of
            field, 155–157
event.preventDefault() method, 155
Events
    App component, 150
    communication
        communicate with child
            component, 161–163
        communicate with parent
            component, 164–166
    form "increment()"/"increment",
        151, 152
    increment() method, 149, 150
    inject() method, 167–169, 171
    MyCounter component, 150
    provide() method, 167–169, 171
    v-on directive, 149
event.target.value, 157

F

fetch(url) method, 183, 281
filter() method, 187, 197, 333, 334
focus() method, 202, 203

GPSR Compliance

The European Union's (EU) General Product Safety Regulation (GPSR) is a set of rules that requires consumer products to be safe and our obligations to ensure this.

If you have any concerns about our products, you can contact us on

ProductSafety@springernature.com

In case Publisher is established outside the EU, the EU authorized representative is:

Springer Nature Customer Service Center GmbH
Europaplatz 3
69115 Heidelberg, Germany